Renee Hartfield

writing your way

A 40-Day Path of Self-Discovery

Writing Your Way: A 40-Day Path of Self-Discovery
Copyright © 2022 by Renée Hartleib

First paperback edition August 2022
HeartWrite Press

ISBN 978-1-7781979-0-1 (paperback)
ISBN 978-1-7781979-1-8 (ebook)

Requests for information should be addressed to:
renee@reneehartleib.com

All rights reserved. No part of this book may be used or reproduced in any manner whatsoever without prior written permission except in the case of brief quotations embodied in reviews.

Cover and interior design: Annemieke Beemster Leverenz

For my daughter, Sadie—
your path and your strength inspire me.

aug 2023

Dear Victoria,
So grateful to connect with you. Thank you for your support!

writing your way

A 40-Day Path of Self-Discovery

Renée

How This Book Began

"What nine months does for the embryo
Forty early mornings
Will do for your growing awareness."

—RUMI

In February of 2017, I created something called *The 40-Day Writing Project*. The idea had come to me in a dream, and I remember waking up and stumbling to my desk to write it down. I had goosebumps everywhere; it was a full-body YES.

I sent a note to my writing mentoring clients and website subscribers, explaining the idea. They would receive an email from me every day for 40 days. Each day's letter would have a mini-essay about writing, creativity, and the things that stop us from creating, plus a writing prompt.

My idea was met with an immediate and passionate welcome. So many people seemed eager for the chance to devote 20 or 30 minutes to themselves every day and to have a directed contemplative practice arrive in their inbox each morning.

Less than a week after the initial idea came to me, we had begun. This short timeline meant that I was creating the project alongside the people who were waiting to receive my morning letters, often only two or three days ahead of them! I remember getting up at 3:30 every morning and writing feverishly until I had to wake my daughter for school. It was an utterly magical time in my life, one where I trusted the yes and watched the words fly out of my fingers.

What I couldn't know then is how profoundly this practice would impact people's lives. I offered the Project over and over, each time with a new group. And as its reach widened, the letters began to arrive from people telling me about their experiences and the kind of meaningful change a 40-day practice had initiated. Their words and experiences blew me away. You can read some of their testimonials in the Reviews section at the back of the book.

What I have learned is that when we gift ourselves time and space, tune out the external world, and listen within, we're making space for inner guidance. And this guidance—

this wisdom that lives within each of us—can transform our lives. Full stop.

It's this knowing that has propelled me to write this book. In a world where we are manipulated to find happiness through consumerism and encouraged to constantly distract ourselves, getting quiet and seeking inner truths is a radical activity. And on a planet that is increasingly chaotic and at odds, structured practices that provide us with a sense of groundedness and peace are essential.

Did you know that the number 40 is sacred across the world's cultures and religions? It shows up in Jewish, Islamic, Christian, Hindu, Buddhist, and Sikh texts, traditions, and practices. In a time where divisiveness seems the norm, I love the thought of bringing people together, using a spiritual number that humanity shares.

For some of you, the idea of doing anything for 40 days straight might feel daunting. I understand that. Many of us already feel stretched. We're also constantly told that our attention spans have shrunk to the size of a goldfish. I don't buy it. We humans are magnificent creatures with the ability to focus, reflect deeply, and act with integrity.

And not just the ability, but the desire! I see a hunger in people to move beyond the myriad distractions of our modern life, seek deeper meaning, and discover what is theirs to contribute to our world.

When you clear time for yourself every day and reflect through writing, you grant yourself a pause in an otherwise busy and distracted life. And it's in this pause that you can hear your own truth and develop the capacity to choose responses that are more in line with who you are and what you actually want.

If you commit, these daily pauses add up and ultimately have the power to change your life, positively affect the lives of those around you, and even impact the broader world.

This book will guide you through 40 days of reflection and self-discovery. My wish for you is that it shines light on what is within you longing to be created, rewards you with insight into what has been holding you back, and gifts you with new and inspiring tools to move toward your most closely held desires and dreams.

THIS BOOK IS FOR YOU IF…

- you crave time alone
- you want to get to know yourself a little more deeply
- you are interested in exploring your creativity
- you're searching for more meaning in your life
- you're curious about your own potential
- you want to tend to your heart and your spirit
- you'd like to help make the world a better place and are wondering what your unique contribution might be

You don't have to be a writer, or consider yourself a writer, to benefit from this book. You are simply using writing as the tool to go within and support reflection.

Getting Ready

The time you make for yourself and your own writing over the next 40 days creates a daily pause (perhaps a much-needed one!) for you to both be yourself *and* be with yourself.

Interrupting the "doing" of life for even a short period of time each day is powerful stuff. But the magic of this process is not contained in the words or the writing prompts of this book.

The magic will come as you put your own time and effort in. Wait until you see what happens! You may have slow and quiet realizations; you may have lightning bolt epiphanies; you may also have a growing awareness of the seeds for future creations that live in you, just waiting to be watered and tended and then released into the world.

Here are a few tips to help you get ready for the days ahead:

Commit.
You'll get the most out of the experience if you can make a commitment to 40 consecutive days (yes, that includes weekends!). This initiates a new habit or routine, one where you're prioritizing yourself.

Same time every day.
It's important that you don't try to fit the writing in *when you can find time*. We all know what happens then! Set a time, preferably the same time every day. Put it in your calendar and stick to it, the same way you would be on time for a meeting with another person.

Make it special.
Writing in the same place every day also really helps! Do you have a cozy spot where you won't be interrupted, or can you create one? Consider what else you can do to make this time special: Light a candle? Brew a type of tea you normally don't drink? Put on comfy clothes?

Respect yourself.
To add to a sense of sacredness, remember to shut the door

if you're in a room that has one, and turn off or silence any device that will beep or buzz at you. I personally love writing by hand, but I know this isn't for everyone. If you are writing on your computer, set up a special folder for your work and turn off notifications so you won't be distracted by incoming emails.

Once you're on a roll, it might be tempting to do more than one day in a sitting, but the process works best when you allow it to unfold one topic and one piece of writing at a time. This gives you time to mull over what has come up for you. Be prepared for fresh insights and ideas to come *after* you've finished your daily writing. If you don't already, consider carrying a notebook to jot down these late arrivals.

And if you miss a day because you're sick or because life got turned upside down, don't be hard on yourself.

I'm excited for you! Your 40 days await you. Enjoy every step of the path ahead.

Day 1

"I argued with my soul for a long time before I came to know it as my wisest self, my compass that would direct me to a different kind of safety, an inner stability that far surpassed anything the noise in my head could imagine. Getting quiet enough to hear the voice of the soul became my practice."

—ELIZABETH LESSER

This book gives you an opportunity, for a short period of time every day, to tune out the external world and tune in to yourself. This is the self you were born with. It's not your personality and it's not your upbringing and it's not your career or how you identify in the broader world (e.g., librarian, parent, non-binary, gay, shy, etc.). Some might call it your soul, your spirit, or your essence. It is the quiet "being" part of you, the self beyond any of life's doingness. The inner, truest version of you. Who you are at your core.

The writing exercises in the days ahead will encourage you to adopt an attitude of kind and passionate curiosity and respect for yourself and your life. What you find out might make you feel squirmy, uncomfortable, nervous, or even ecstatic. What you hear from inside might also make you realize that something in your life needs to change. Learning to be gentle with whatever you uncover is so important.

Today is the start. Today, you commit to 40 consecutive days of peering inside and writing about what you find. Take a moment to feel proud of yourself and to quiet the internal voice that might be saying you don't have time for this, the one that doubts you can do it or that is giving you the stink-eye before you even begin. We'll talk more about this inner critic—and we all have one—in the days ahead.

Take a deep breath. And let's begin.

YOUR WRITING

> *"Whatever you can do,*
> *Or dream you can do,*
> *Begin it.*
> *Boldness has genius, power, and magic in it.*
> *Begin it now."*
>
> —GOETHE

For this very first activity, write about where you are in life right now. Create a snapshot of how your life feels at this moment in time. Remember, no one is going to read this but you, so be honest and real.

Here are a few questions to guide you:

What's happening for you? What's not happening (that you wish was happening)? What is consuming you? What is irritating you? What is bringing you joy?

Are you at a crossroads? Are you grieving? Are you dreaming?

What are you curious about? What do you want to learn? Are you trying to pivot toward or away from something?

Day 2

*"Nothing, no one, is too small to matter.
What you do is going to make a difference."*

—MADELEINE L'ENGLE

Many years ago now, I discovered a wonderful book in a used bookstore called *If You Want to Write: A Book About Art, Independence, and Spirit*. It was written in 1938 by a woman named Brenda Ueland, who was an American journalist and writing teacher. I picked it up because I'm a writer, but so much of the book's wisdom relates to all of us, regardless of our vocation.

One of the very first assertions in her book is this: "Everyone is talented, original, and has something important to say."

Read that line again. And let it soak in. YOU are talented, you are original, and you have something important to say.

If this very idea makes you blush or scoff or want to bury your head in the sand, that's okay. You may want it to be true, or suspect it is true, but your life hasn't borne this idea out yet. Or you may already know this, and in that case, good for you!

Ueland spent years and years teaching a large and diverse class at a Minnesota YWCA. She said: "There were all kinds of people—men and women, rich and poor, erudite and uneducated, highbrow professors and little servant girls so shy that it would take months to arouse in them the courage to try a sentence or two."

And what Ueland found was that when people were writing from a true place inside of them—what she called "the true self," the centre of all "originality, talent, honour, courage, and cheerfulness"—the stories they told were 100 percent unique and often absolutely bold and riveting.

YOUR WRITING

I want you to take Brenda Ueland's statement and break it down into three parts, writing answers to the questions I pose below.

You are talented.
What were you taught about talent growing up? What were

you told about your own talents? Do you believe you have unique talents? If so, what are they?

You are original.
What do you think it means to be "original"? Do you believe you are original? Why or why not?

You have something important to say.
Do you believe this to be true about YOU? Why or why not? Do you have any inklings about what you have to say?

Lastly, what might be possible if you believed Brenda Ueland's words?

Now, after you're finished your writing, make a point of returning to this phrase a few times today and repeat it to yourself. **"I am talented, original, and have something important to say."**

Think of it as a sacred incantation, one that may protect you against some of the critical judgments that can arise quickly when we go off the beaten path, stop listening to what the rest of the world expects from us (for even a minute), and dare to look within.

Day 3

*"Creativity is our birthright.
It is an integral part of being human, as basic as
walking, talking, and thinking."*

—JOHN DAIDO LOORI

When people find out what I do, there is a common response. "A writer?" they exclaim, and their eyes light up. Often, this is followed by "I wish I could write, but I'm not creative at all."

You've likely heard others (or yourself!) say things like this. I call it "The Myth about Creativity." Why the word "myth"? Because creativity is an essential part of who we are as human beings; it's not just special for some.

Did you know that there is no word for "creative" in the Tibetan language? The closest translation is the word "natural." Tibetans equate being human with being creative. To them, the two are one and the same.

Now, compare this to Western teachings about creativity, where we learn that some people are more creative than others and the "creative" ones become artists or musicians or writers. In reality, these people are no more creative; they are simply using their creativity to make a living.

If you've bought this line of thought and truly don't see yourself as creative, consider this: You use creativity every day too. You're just not getting paid for it! In the run of an average day, you tap into your natural creativity when you get dressed in the morning, when you tell stories to other people, when you make a meal, when you choose music for a playlist, and even when you're emailing or texting.

These aren't great works of art, but being creative doesn't mean you are always producing great works of art. That is part of the myth.

Have you ever noticed how easygoing very young children are with their art and the things they make? There is no judgment and often no "finished" product. If a painting doesn't turn out the way they expected, they do another one. Their creative stream is endless, and they inherently know this. As Pablo Picasso once said, "Every child is an artist, the problem is staying an artist when you grow up."

Your creative stream is always flowing under the surface. It is part of who you are as a human being. Remember this today.

YOUR WRITING

I'd like you to explore what you have been taught about creativity and how you feel about the creativity that lives in you. Here are some questions to guide you:

What were you taught about creativity as a child?

What were you told about your own creativity?

How do you feel about yourself as a creative person?

Write about some of the "easy" ways that creativity shows up in your life.

What creative activities are part of your daily life? These may be things that are so normal and natural that you don't even consider them creative. Does it show up in the meals you cook? The photographs you take? The types of hats you wear? The way you dress? The type of gifts you give others?

It's not uncommon for the critical part of us to make an appearance in an exercise like this. You might hear that negative voice in your head saying something like "You don't have a creative bone in your body," or "You're fooling yourself," or "Stop bragging." We'll talk more about the inner critic in the days ahead. For now, if you can, simply name this voice "the critic" and keep moving forward.

Day 4

"Movement is medicine."

—CLARA HUGHES

As a kid, I intuitively understood that when I played outside and moved my body, I felt better. After a back injury in my teens, I lost this knowing and for a number of years lived more in the mental realm. I missed that connection with my physical self though, and in my thirties, sought to get back in touch with my body— first through yoga, then through working out and running, and now through long-form walking and pickleball games.

The rediscovery that moving my body is essential to my emotional well-being has been such a gift. Especially through the pandemic years, physical activity grounded me and flooded my body with endorphins, making me feel more resilient and alive.

The movement that is most non-negotiable to me now is walking. Walks with the dog, walks on the beach, walks with friends and family—each type of walk raises my spirits, but the ones that incite creativity or inspire revelation are often my long walks alone.

I'm not the only one who feels that walking loosens something within. Myriad artists and thinkers over time have made links between walking and "solving." Nietzsche believed that all truly great thoughts were conceived while walking. Virginia Woolf literally "paced" out the plots of her novels as she walked the streets of London. Charles Dickens walked up to 20 miles after his daily writing session and once told a friend: "If I couldn't walk fast and far, I should explode and perish."

In modern times, there are plenty of creative types who talk about the link between healing and movement. Cheryl Strayed, author of *Wild: Lost and Found on the Pacific Crest Trail*, even says that walking saved her soul. High praise indeed.

There is actual science behind the experiences of these writers and thinkers. In 2014, a Stanford University study revealed that creative thinking improves while a person is walking and shortly thereafter. And the good news is that the effects are the same whether you are in the great outdoors or on an indoor treadmill. If you aren't able to walk, and I know that not everyone can, there are also physical and emotional benefits to other forms of movement.

For me, the most powerful element of any movement practice is the energy shift that occurs. I've proven to myself over and over again that taking an hour to go for a walk, do yoga, or go to the gym actually makes me more productive, alert, and energetic. It also grounds me and puts complex emotions or situations into perspective. Can't beat that!

YOUR WRITING

I want you to write about the role of movement in your life. Allow these questions to guide you:

Is movement part of your daily routine? If so, describe what you do and the impact it has on you.

If you have another daily practice that grounds and enlivens you, write about what it is and how it helps you.

If you don't have a daily movement practice, would you consider adding one for these 40 days? Write about how it feels to contemplate this and what kind of physical movement you might add to your day.

(This doesn't mean you need to carve out more time alone—your movement practice can include partners, pets, or children! Anything that gets you up and out and moving.)

Day 5

*"Talk to yourself like you would
to someone you love."*

—BRENÉ BROWN

I've dropped a few hints about the critics that live in our heads, but today is devoted to investigating this inner saboteur of our most tender hopes, dreams, and longings.

First things first: we *all* have an inner critical voice. No one is immune or exempt. But we all have our own unique version of this voice that is connected to how we were raised.

Psychologists say that our inner critic forms in childhood as we ingest parental and societal messages about how to be in the world. When we are cautioned about behaviours that might cause us to be ostracized or rejected, we internalize that information and create a belief system of our own. Basically, the role of the inner critic is to spare us shame by warning us when we begin to enter potentially "dangerous territory."

It's ironic that something that developed to help us avoid the negative emotion of shame actually causes shame. Our inner critic shouts, calls us names, and is often downright vicious. This part of us is also sneaky, crafting critical words to sound like the truth. The truth that other people are too polite to say; that's what we tell ourselves.

Our inner critic likes to give opinions about almost everything: how we look, the work we do, the work we don't do, what we just said, what we didn't say, and what kind of parents and partners and people we are. Our critic is convinced we're not smart enough, attractive enough, cool enough, creative enough, or organized enough. In fact, according to our critic, we're just not "enough," period!

I'll bet your inner critic has already jumped in with an opinion or two about this 40-day journey *and* the writing you've done so far. Am I right?

Just listen to the things your critic says and imagine yourself saying the same things to a family member or good friend. You would likely *never* talk to someone else in the same way. Now imagine putting the words of your critic into the mouth of anyone close to you (or even not that close to you!). You would be so shocked and angry if another person talked to you the way you talk to yourself!

Here are five things I've discovered about the critic:

- **Your critic learned everything it knows from other people.** This voice is a product of how you were trained. That means that it reflects the fears and beliefs of those who raised you but does not necessarily match who you are or what you deeply believe.
- **Your critic is trying to protect you from all the things you were taught to fear.** It just doesn't have a clue how to do that. Why not? See below.
- **Your critic is very young and very terrified.** It learned everything it knows at a young age and has zero adult discernment. It is constantly on guard, trying to protect you from anything it perceives to be dangerous (which sometimes feels like everything!).
- **Your critic is an excellent impersonator.** It might be young, but it knows how to parrot your parents or your elders. After all, that's who taught it. This is why your critic can sound like an authority or a truth-teller.
- **You have agency when it comes to the critic.** I know it doesn't feel like it, but you can actually learn to control this dialogue in your head. You are the adult. This means

you can recognize your inner critic is young, terrified, and misguided and try to soothe this part of you.

If soothing is out of the question, simply remembering to notice and label the critical voice in our heads as "the inner critic" can be hugely important and beneficial. This reminds us that what we're hearing is a perverse kind of protection, not truth, and this knowledge can lessen its power and destructive impact.

YOUR WRITING

A two-parter today:

Part One:
To separate this critical voice from the essence of you, I'd like you to write about YOUR inner critic as if they were a real person. *Remember, this isn't you.* When I did this exercise many years ago at a writing workshop, I discovered that my inner critic is a bit of a slimeball— greasy hair, bad complexion, terrible slouchy posture. He was full of bluster and bravado, but not terribly smart. He reminded me of the "man behind the curtain" in the Wizard of Oz. This was really helpful to know!

Here are some questions to guide this piece of writing:

Does your critic have a gender? What do they wear? How do they move in the world? What does their voice sound like? How do they "hook" you? How do they attempt to convince you that what they are saying is the truth?

Write down all the descriptive details that will really bring your critic to life. Do you recognize any of their characteristics from people who may have influenced the way you think about yourself?

Part Two:
After you leave the pages of this book and your own writing today, set an intention to notice when your critic makes an appearance. Try to isolate the voice and separate it from you by labelling it whenever you hear it. At the first unkind thought toward yourself, simply say, "Ah, there's the critic," and move on. Continue doing this every time the critical voice attempts to have a say.

If you're up for a bit more writing, consider jotting down what the critic says to you. It can be enlightening to see its opinions on paper. Also, note when it is most likely to pipe up. When is it especially loud? How does it make you feel? Do you already have strategies for dealing with your critic? Write those down too, and explore what's working and what's not.

Day 6

"Transformation doesn't ask that you stop being you. It demands that you find a way back to the authenticity and strength that's already inside you. You only have to bloom."

—CHERYL STRAYED

When I was a teenager, I liked nothing more than to blast my music. The louder, the better. In the basement, in the living room, in the car, in my bedroom. My poor parents. I can remember my mother lamenting, "Can't we just have a little peace and quiet?" I had no idea what she was talking about.

I do now. In the mornings when I sit down to write, I am very aware of how rich and textured the silence is. At previous times in my life, this kind of silence would have felt empty and dangerous. I would have wanted to fill it. But now, it feels essential to my life and my writing practice.

I didn't get here overnight. My inner critic has always been active, but never more so than when a little quiet descended. This meant I needed to keep myself busy and distracted. I read until I fell asleep, the radio was always on, and it was hard to sit still. At the time, this seemed like simple self-preservation, because when the distractions stopped, my critic attacked hard.

One summer in my early thirties, things came to a head after two back-to-back injuries plus a terrible flu. I was stuck in bed, unable to stay busy, unable to distract myself. Unleashed, my inner critical demon swooped and screeched, dropping its hideous bombs of self-loathing as I lay unprotected in bed. The assault was relentless.

The critic attacks wore me down to the point where I started to feel angry. This was all happening in my own head—surely, I had some agency here! I began to wonder if it might be possible to teach myself how to be okay with life's quiet moments rather than rushing to fill them. Could I school myself in intentional quiet so that the next time I was sick or injured, I wouldn't be ambushed?

With this question at the forefront of my mind, I challenged myself to stop the constant doing. I wanted to learn how to be quiet and still so I didn't have to avoid being quiet and still! The very thought terrified me. I knew I had to start small. "What about 10 minutes?" I wondered. "Surely I can do nothing for only 10 minutes a day?"

Ha! This was torture. You should know I wasn't attempting to meditate or do any fancy breathing techniques. I was simply sitting still with my eyes open. And in a beautiful place too—I had chosen a large public garden close to where I lived—but wow, was it ever hard! I couldn't stop looking at my watch, plus I had to contend with the critical voice telling me all of this was a waste of time.

But something magical and kind of mysterious happened when I sat on that park bench, the same one every day. I slowly became present to the world. The fountain in front of me. The statue of the woman on top of the fountain, gently and steadfastly pouring water from an urn. The people who walked by. The other people who sat down and looked at the fountain too.

And as I became more present, I started to feel calmer and more peaceful. I noticed that the critical voice seemed more distant, almost muffled, like I'd created a bubble where it couldn't enter. I can see now, in retrospect, that I had been maintaining a manic pace in an attempt to avoid the critic, but that my frantic busyness had kept me from something else that existed inside of me.

A place of presence, a place of peace. What a revelation!

YOUR WRITING

Write about your experiences of "doing" versus "being." What are the differences between these two states for you?

Do you keep yourself busy and distracted? What purpose does it serve? And what might it be keeping you from?

I'd also like you to explore the role of quiet and silence in your life. Do you fill the quiet moments, or are you able to relish them?

Lastly, if you recognize that you are one of those people—like I was—who needs to stay constantly busy (for your own unique, possibly unconscious, reasons!), I'd like to challenge you to commit to doing nothing for 10 minutes per day. Try this for even one week and see what happens. Notice any shifts and write about your experience.

Day 7

*"Self-care is never a selfish act—it is
simply good stewardship of the only gift I have,
the gift I was put on earth to offer others.
Anytime we can listen to our true self and give
the care it requires, we do it not only for ourselves,
but for the many others whose lives we touch."*

—PARKER PALMER

Have you ever wondered how different the world would be if we were taught that taking care of ourselves must always come before taking care of others? What if we learned, from a young age, that only in valuing ourselves and putting our own self-care first will we ever be able to effectively care for anyone else?

Unfortunately, as you well know, this is not happening! Women, especially, receive strong societal messages about prioritizing other people's needs over their own. This training starts very young, so it's no wonder that when young girls become women (especially if they are in heterosexual relationships), they think it's normal to work all day outside the home, but still be the ones responsible for most household and family duties.

Yet, when you get on a plane, they show a video of putting your own oxygen mask on before helping anyone else, even your own child! This really is the perfect metaphor for the importance of self-care. If we don't look after ourselves, we won't have the "oxygen" (the health or energy) to care for others. Seems like a no-brainer, but sadly this advice tends to stay on airplanes.

Here's what I think self-care is: Giving ourselves the same kind of care and attention we so freely give to others. And like Parker Palmer in the quote above, I believe that this care and attention and love must be directed at the truest part of who we are.

This is not the part of us that is the family superhero, making lunches, mending clothes, tending to aging parents, meeting with teachers, and going grocery shopping. This is not the part that is the office star, staying late, writing the best reports, meeting every deadline, and routinely exceeding everyone's expectations. Our true self is not the performer, and it's not who we were taught to be.

This true self is the part of us I wrote about on Day 1—the quiet, soulful, "being" part. Caring for this deep inner self means making time to connect. Connect and then listen for what it has to say. Intentionally listening for this voice and then attending to what it expresses is at the heart of self-care.

YOUR WRITING

I'd like you to imagine that this truest part of you is a small child who has been entrusted to your care. As my mother used to say to anyone who showed up at the house to give me a lift: "Now drive carefully! You've got a precious cargo." Our inner selves *are* precious and they need and deserve nurturing and care.

Today, I'd like you to tenderly pose some questions to this inner part of you:

What's the best way for me to take care of you?

How do you most want to spend your time?

What is important to you? What are you missing? What do you need?

How are you feeling?

Whatever comes up, write it down. Show this inner part of you that you're listening and that you respect what it has to say.

Day 8

"Lift up your eyes upon this day breaking for you.
Give birth again to the dream."

—MAYA ANGELOU

I am a morning person. It hasn't always been this way. As teenagers, my sister and I would sleep in until 11 o'clock in the summer, then roll out of bed and watch TV game shows before we even saw the light of the day. Oh my, how times have changed!

My father was my first inspiration when it came to a love of the quiet morning hours. Sometimes, on holidays, I would get up early with him and we would go "exploring," checking out a new place while the world was still. My dad always seemed so excited and grateful to be alive in those early mornings, and it was through his example that I learned each day can be a fresh start.

By my late thirties, I had also figured out that mornings can be a time of great productivity, especially for projects that were my own. I remember hearing the writer Jean Shinoda Bolen talk about how she managed to write books while still working as a busy psychiatrist and Jungian analyst. Her secret? Getting up at 4 AM. That way, she was able to put in at least three hours on her own writing before starting her workday.

I began the practice of rising early to work on my fiction writing when I was both a new parent and a new business owner. It was the only way I managed to get short stories written and published.

When I started working as a writing mentor, I remember being afraid to even suggest morning writing to my clients. So many people I knew thought I was crazy for getting up so early. It felt like too much to ask of anyone. But then, I had a conversation with a friend who was "stuck"— she wanted to write but it just wasn't happening.

"By the time I get home from work and eat supper and clean up, I'm exhausted. I just want to zone out in front of a show."

"How about the mornings?" I asked.

"I'm not a morning person," she said. "I can only write at night."

"Except you're not writing at night because you're too tired," I pushed. "Have you ever tried the morning?"

"Well, no, but I don't think it would go very well."

"What do you do in the mornings?"

"I have coffee. I take a shower. I get dressed. I go to work."

"Do you sit down when you drink your coffee?"

She nodded. "I like a few minutes of peace before my partner gets up and everything starts."

"So, what if you had your notebook and pen beside your coffee cup? What if you wrote for 10 minutes before you started your day?"

She seemed dubious and didn't promise she'd try, but a week later, I got a euphoric email extolling the virtues of morning writing. "I love it!" she exclaimed. "I can't believe I never tried it before. What an amazing way to start my day!"

YOUR WRITING

Do some gentle inquiry about what time of day you feel most alive, most yourself, and most joyful. Here are a few questions to guide your writing reflection:

When is your best time of day? Why is it the best? How do you feel? What do you choose to do during this "best" time?

If this time of day is currently used to care for others, what might need to shift in your life to make sure that you are assigning some of your "best" time to yourself?

When have you been doing the writing assignments in this book? Do you have a specific time? Does the time you've chosen work for you?

When you listen within, is there a better time?

Day 9

"First forget inspiration. Habit is more dependable. Habit will sustain you whether you're inspired or not. Habit will help you finish and polish your stories. Inspiration won't. Habit is persistence in practice."

—OCTAVIA E. BUTLER

There's a lot of information out there about inspiration and how it's necessary to be inspired before you can create anything. The very premise of this book—showing up for yourself and writing for 40 days straight—flies in the face of that. If you were waiting to be inspired, you might show up for two or three days, but likely not for 40 in a row!

Personally, I prefer the advice of other creatives who believe in inspiration but know that you have to put in the work of showing up consistently first. I'll write more about this idea tomorrow. But first, a story!

One day, while doing my post-workout stretch at the gym, I saw one of the trainers lacing up his sneakers. His shift was ending and he was about to do his own exercise routine.

"What kind of workout today?" I asked him.

"Ah, today's a slack day," he said.

"Slack?"

"Yep, I haven't been feeling very motivated lately, so I'm letting myself have slack workouts. You know, when you still do it, but your heart's not in it? I know it's going to turn around, but I just have to wait it out."

I nodded, already seeing the parallel to any form of commitment.

And then he nailed it: "It's one of the most important things for people to learn when they start working out. You can't stop on a day you don't feel it. Otherwise you lose your momentum. A slack workout is always better than no workout because your body maintains what you've achieved so far."

Bingo.

This concept is easily understood when it is applied to any form of physical exercise, but I would argue it's exactly the same for any kind of discipline. During these 40 days, you may already have noticed that missing or skipping one day can easily turn into two or three days—it's a slippery slope.

And any longer than three days is really playing with fire, because those are the times when it's easiest for the critic to creep in. "I told you! I knew you wouldn't be able to do this. You've always had a problem with commitment. Not to mention that your writing is a complete waste of time." On and on the critic will go, if we give it even a partly opened door to wedge a foot into.

The solution? In addition to setting aside a consistent time for your writing, do your best not to let anything get in the way of you showing up at the time you've decided upon. Make it as important as all the other things you prioritize.

And then, on the days when you don't feel it or aren't inspired at all or are pulled in the direction of other responsibilities, keep going. Write anyway. Think of it as your "slack workout," and pat yourself on the back for keeping your momentum going.

YOUR WRITING

Today's writing exercise: I want you to write without purpose or destination, using what is called "stream of consciousness" writing. Record whatever comes into your head, moment to moment, as fast as you can. I don't want you to wonder if what you are writing makes sense. I don't want you to wonder if it is "good." And I don't even want you to think about spelling or grammar.

Let yourself roam wild and free with your words. If you are writing with a pen on paper, keep the pen moving the entire time. Don't stop. If you are typing on a computer or an old-fashioned typewriter, keep your hands moving. Don't think, don't fret, don't plan. Just write. And see what happens.

Writing without purpose or destination can be very freeing. You may be surprised where it takes you. It's also a great way to practise not being hard on yourself. When there's no time to edit, the critic can't jump in.

Day 10

"The power that makes grass grow, fruit ripen, and guides the birds in flight is in us all."

—ANZIA YEZIERSKA

You don't have to consider yourself an artist to read *The Artist's Way* by Julia Cameron. You also don't have to be religious or spiritual, even though at the core of Cameron's teachings is this belief: a higher power exists and it likes to help humans.

She speaks of this higher power as an unseen but powerful and cooperative force that we can harness for our creative endeavours. From the first page of her book, she calls this force "God" but acknowledges this word is loaded for some and suggests we use whatever term feels most comfortable—divine, source, flow, goddess, creator. Cameron adds that if you don't want to call it anything, you don't have to. "You don't have to understand electricity to use it," she says.

Julia Cameron isn't the only one who believes that unseen forces can assist humans on their creative paths. Poet William Blake called this spiritual electricity the "Imagination" and said it was from the creator, whom he called the Poetic Genius: "He who loves feels love descend into him and if he has wisdom, may perceive it is from the Poetic Genius."

In a similar vein, the premise of Elizabeth Gilbert's book *Big Magic* is that we humans have a "supernatural, mystical, inexplicable, surreal, divine, transcendent, and otherworldly" force at our fingertips, accessible if we simply choose to focus and show up for our creative work.

It's not just writers who believe they are tapping into something greater than themselves when they create. Grammy-winning singer Sara Bareilles says this: "I believe that the universe responds very positively to the gesture of making space for creativity." She goes on to say that she believes that when we create, we are channelling something, "connecting into some greater network that has been around long before we were here and will continue to be around long after we're gone."

And famous modern dancer, teacher, and choreographer Martha Graham believed that this energy—which can either be accepted or blocked—is used to create unique expressions for every single person. "If you block it, it will never exist through any other medium and be lost. The world will not have it. It is not yours to determine how good it is; nor how it compares with other expressions. It is your business to keep the channel open."

I can attest to what these other artists are expressing here. Time and time again, I've felt supported and sustained by an unseen energy that seems to appear when I show up for my creative projects. As my own level of commitment increases, I feel this energy—what I call the "universe" or the "friendly universe" (to remind me of its benevolent nature)—picking up the pace, accompanying me, and directing me as I move forward.

YOUR WRITING

Today, we are going to explore this idea of an unseen cooperative energy that helps us work toward our creative and life goals.

Do you believe in this idea? If you do, what do you call it?

Write about a time in your life where you experienced this energy helping you. What did it look like and feel like to have this kind of help?

If you don't believe in this concept of a friendly unseen force, write about what you believe instead.

Also, consider what it might take for you to try this idea on. As Julia Cameron advised, can you experiment with this "electricity" even if you don't understand it?

Day 11

"Much sheer effort goes into avoiding truth: left to itself, it sweeps in like the tide."

—FAY WELDON

On Day 7, I wrote about taking the time to connect to the truest part of ourselves and intentionally listening for its wisdom. But have you ever noticed that inner wisdom sometimes arises even when we don't ask or aren't actively listening?

People sometimes refer to this as their "little voice," as in *"There was a little voice that told me we should break up"* or *"I knew I should have taken that other job, but this one had a better salary, benefits, and a pension."*

There is wisdom in this voice. It sounds quite different from our inner critic, more calm and grounded, and it seems to know us well. It talks to us about our current situations and sometimes suggests changes related to work, relationships, fitness, or health. Other times, it incites us to remember our big dreams, the ones we wanted more than anything but haven't achieved yet. Writing a book. Volunteering. Making art. Running for public office. Taking acting classes. Walking the Camino. Going back to school.

I believe that this voice of truth, this inner knowing, is nothing less than our soul attempting to communicate with us. And what you're doing in these 40 days is listening. You are tuning out distractions, you are focusing within, and you are creating space for the most inner you to speak.

And when it communicates with us, I've found that our inner truth-teller, this "soul voice," does not concern itself with trivialities. It doesn't chime in about what to make for supper or what to wear on Friday night. It's not at all concerned about promotions or paying off our student loans. And it couldn't care less about our pension and investments.

If you're listening, your soul voice will state surely and succinctly what is in the deepest, most private places of your heart. It knows you better than anyone else and will speak to you about who you really are. It might tell you that you deserve a partner who treats you better. It might encourage you to find another job. It might suggest that you should spend more time doing what you love.

DAY 11

It speaks profoundly, but it sometimes says very inconvenient things, this voice. Things that cause a lot of trouble. And that's why people work hard to drown it out. They drink it away. They talk it away. They shop it away. They Netflix it away. They Instagram and TikTok it away.

But still the soul voice rises up through the layers of distraction to speak to us. How strong it is! How brave! It wants big things for us. It wants us to love and be loved. It wants us to have lives of meaning and joy and truth. It might even tell us that we have something unique and meaningful to give to others and the world.

YOUR WRITING

Throughout our lives, this voice of undiluted truth speaks, but if the message feels too large or difficult for us to take action on, we often don't heed its wisdom.

Consider these questions in your writing today:

Has the "little voice" or your "soul voice" made an unbidden appearance in your life? Write about when and what happened.

How do you feel about this voice inside you?

What is this truth-teller telling you now?

How do you feel about what it is asking for or reminding you of?

If this notion of a soul voice is new to you, just play with the idea of it. Try to be open. Get quiet, listen, and see what you hear. Make sure to write down what it says.

Day 12

*"Someone once told me that fear and courage
are like lightning and thunder; they both start out
at the same time, but the fear travels faster
and arrives sooner. If we just wait a moment,
the requisite courage will be along shortly."*

—LAWRENCE BLOCK

As you start to tune inside more intentionally, you may feel inspired and excited about what you're discovering. You might also feel anxious or overwhelmed or scared. Today, we are going to shed light on one of the main stumbling blocks to actually taking action on our innermost hopes and dreams.

The F word. FEAR. That unpleasant and constricting emotion that stops so many of us from doing what we deeply desire.

I want to share a story with you about a bit of a light bulb moment I had about fear.

The setting: An Astrology Reading.

Important information for you to know: At the time of this reading, I had not settled into a career and was instead juggling a number of different jobs. My secret ambition was to be a writer, but I was stymied by... you can probably guess what!

I'll let the story tell you the rest.

♥

Astrologer: (*Smiling and peering intently at my chart*) So, you do a lot of public speaking, a lot of teaching. You like to be up in front of people, sharing what you know with them. (*She said this like it was a given; there wasn't even a question in that remark.*)

Me: (*Aghast*) No! (*And thinking, oh great, this person is a total quack.*)

Astrologer: (*Looking at her chart more closely and then back up at me, obviously wondering if I was an imposter with the wrong birth date.*) You don't?

DAY 12

Me: I'm terrified of public speaking. Always have been. It's my worst nightmare to be "up in front of people." I hate being the centre of attention. (*I stop short of saying that I blush ferociously when I have to talk at any kind of a meeting and my heart pounds relentlessly when I have to introduce myself in a group.*)

Astrologer: Well, you should. More than that, actually. You have to. This is who you are. (*Pointing to the evidence—my chart.*) You're meant to share what you know in some sort of very public way. And you will. You just have to get over the fear, and when you're free of it, you'll be able to do more of what you are really good at.

♥

To say this conversation was a revelation is a gross understatement. Partly it was her passionate conviction that I was missing out on a huge part of who I was. But even more important was what she said about fear: That I could be free of it. That the fear wasn't me.

This was a totally new spin.

As the child of an anxious parent, I thought of fear as an integral part of who I was. Fear had grown with me, literally in the marrow of my bones. But the astrologer seemed to be saying that I had a choice. I could address my fear as the interloper it was. Not me. Just a part of me, and one I could be free of.

Enter a challenge. Our local writers' federation offered a program that paired an emerging writer with someone published. You worked together for many months on a project and at the end you presented your work in a public reading. While I longed to explore myself as a writer, I'd refused to apply because I didn't want dying of fright to be part of the package.

The revelations of my astrology chart made me (sort of) brave. So I applied. And of course, because the universe is like that, I was accepted. And I did the program, all the while dreading the end but forcing myself to practise speaking in front of mirrors and the cat. When it came time, I did the unthinkable; I stood up in front of people and read a story. And you know what? Someone I knew came up to me at the end and said, "Hey, I didn't know you were so good at that."

So good at that? Are you kidding me? Like I'd been public speaking for years and she had just missed the opportunity to see me!

I jumped right on that momentum (if you've got the demon in a chokehold but it's still thrashing, that is *not* the time to let go) and signed up for a series of open mics around the city. I made myself get up and read, over and over again. It worked. I no longer had nightmares about public speaking, and although I was still nervous, it was a lot more comfortable.

DAY 12

I proved to myself I could do it—that the fear was not me.

I've learned something else about fear since that time. I've discovered that when my fear reaction is strong, I can be certain that the thing I want to do is important. As in, aligned with what my soul voice wants. Big fear doesn't crop up around neutral things; the more deeply buried the wish, or the more sweet and tender the longing, the fiercer the fear.

Hmm. Fear as a guidepost then? As a breadcrumb on your path? Let's consider!

YOUR WRITING

What if you began to see your fear as helpful information, not just a stopper? What if you believed that fear could help you by pointing you in the right direction?

Radical stuff!

First: Write about how fear shows up in your life. What are you afraid of? What does fear stop you from doing?

Second: Is there a correlation between these fears and what your soul voice whispers to you?

Last: Does the notion of fear as "helpful information" resonate with you? If so, write about fear as a guidepost on *your* path. Where is it pointing? What do you need courage for?

Day 13

"I have found if you love life, life will love you back."

—ARTHUR RUBINSTEIN

Did you know that research shows that we humans have what's called a "negativity bias"? This means that we are more likely to remember insults over praise, and we tend to make decisions by focusing on what we don't want, rather than on what we do want.

The classic example of the negativity bias in action is the performance appraisal. Our boss gives us gold stars on absolutely every aspect of our job but mentions that one small area needs improvement. What do we fixate on? The one small area. Can we even remember the positive things that were said? Probably not.

It's human nature. And biologically speaking, it makes perfect sense. Paying attention to threats in the environment was literally a matter of life and death when humankind was evolving. People who paid more attention to the negative (danger and threats) were more likely to survive.

So, okay. We're wired this way. Our brains are trying to keep us safe. But in modern times, we don't need the same kind of hyper vigilance. For most of us, there are no sabre-toothed tigers lurking around the corner. Knowing we are not in mortal danger, how do we shift our focus away from scanning for the negatives? And is there something else we can offer ourselves in light of this baked-in negativity bias?

Enter fascinating neuroscience research that proves our brains have what is called "plasticity," meaning they can be rewired. It's actually possible for us to lay new tracks in our brains, ones that lead to positive changes in both our mental and physical health. This means we can train ourselves to pay attention to positive occurrences, rather than being on guard for what is going wrong.

A number of years back, I began a practice of writing down what I felt appreciation or gratitude for first thing every morning. The call of birds in the garden, my daughter's wonderful school, the cup of tea I was drinking, a poem or a song I really loved, the colour of the trees.

Some days gratitude just flowed out of me and I quickly

DAY 13

filled an entire page. Other days it was more of a slog, but what became obvious was that the practice itself was energizing and enlivening. It just made me feel good to do it!

Over the years, I've returned to my gratitude practice over and over again. Even when I'm feeling low, the act of turning toward beauty and goodness always lifts my spirits. My partner and I often start our day like this, saying out loud the things we appreciate or are grateful for.

As we attempt to become more fully ourselves, and as we more purposefully inhabit our lives, there are things that are always going to get in the way—fear, anxiety, doubt, the inner critic. But I've learned there are tools available to us that we can use as an antidote or a salve. Spending time in a state of appreciation or gratitude is one of these.

YOUR WRITING

Write down ten things you appreciate or feel gratitude for. When you've completed your list, pick one of those "appreciations" and expand on it, writing a few paragraphs or even a page about one particular thing.

Additional questions if you want to dig deeper:

What is your experience of the negativity bias in your own life?

What are you attending to? Where are you placing your attention?

Have you discovered your own salve or balm for the things that get in the way of living well, creating, or thriving? Are you actively working to rewire your own brain? If not, could you? How?

Day 14

"When we are told that something is not to be spoken about, we understand this to mean that this something should not exist—should not, cannot, must not, does not exist. In that moment our reality and, consequently, our lives, are distorted; they become shameful and diminished. In some ways, we understand this to mean we should not exist."

—DEENA METZGER

Brené Brown didn't intend to become a "shame researcher." Far from it. She actually started out studying connection. Here's what she learned: Connection to others is what gives our lives meaning and purpose. In fact, it's so important that we spend vast amounts of our energy trying to avoid becoming "disconnected," and huge swaths of time fearing that we are, in some way, unlovable and unworthy of connection.

This feeling at our core that we are unlovable is shame, and it's universal. We all have it. Brown defines shame as an "intensely painful feeling or experience of believing that we are flawed and therefore unworthy of love and belonging."

Even though we all experience shame, most of us don't talk about it, despite the fact that it has massive impacts on the way we live and the decisions we make. The things that make us feel shame are different for every person—appearance, sexuality, mental health, traumatic experiences, age—and it can be triggered when we internalize societal messages.

One of Brené Brown's key messages is that we don't have to let shame wreak havoc on our lives. By recognizing shame and talking about it, rather than burying it, we can heal.

When I first "came out," it was only to myself. There were no Pride parades and there were no parents marching in PFLAG rallies. Back in the '80s, in the place I grew up, it was definitely not okay to be anything other than straight. Heterosexual was normal, so if you weren't straight, there was something wrong with you. And you learned to hide that something.

DAY 14

I only knew of one openly gay person, whom the community ostracized and ridiculed, and I had never heard a positive thing about being gay. But I understood without a shadow of a doubt that I *was* this thing that was so loathed. My journal from the time says things like "I wish I could just be normal," and "I feel disgusting, like I have a horrible curse," and "There's no one to talk to. I feel so alone."

Over the next few years, I hid who I was, continuing to date a boy when my heart wasn't in it while slowly gathering information through books (there was no Internet then!). At around age 20, I made friends with a co-worker who turned out to be a lesbian. We didn't really have much in common, but she did take me to my first gay bar. I remember looking around in happy astonishment at an entire room full of women who were dancing close or holding hands or kissing. I had no idea such a place existed.

And while I was glad to not feel so alone anymore and to know there *were* others like me, and there *were* places they hung out, every time I left the bar to head home, I was filled with a deep sense of shame and confusion. This feeling only intensified when I finally came out to my parents.

At the time, they weren't able to be supportive and gave me the message to not tell anyone, to not act on my feelings, and to continue hiding. I can see now that they too had absorbed society's homophobic conditioning and were trying to protect me from being hurt or hated.

What they were unable to know was how their reactions served to deepen the acute shame I already felt. Their words and behaviour made me feel that my differentness—my truth—was wrong.

Over time, and as cultural norms changed, I found the courage to live who I actually was. It was clear that to continue to pretend I was something I wasn't would make me deeply unhappy. And although I couldn't quite articulate it then, I knew that to deny myself real and true love would harm the deeper "soul" part of me, no matter what anyone else thought or said.

My story has a happy ending—I now share a life and a house and a family with someone wonderful—but it has taken many, many years to get here. That profound sense of shame that I was taught and that I deeply absorbed meant years of suffering and more years of healing. I'm keenly aware that not everyone who was similarly shamed has survived.

YOUR WRITING

Are you able to make a link between the shame you feel and societal messages? For instance, many women feel shame about their weight or body shape because of the types of bodies our culture idealizes. Men often feel ashamed of their feelings because of an extremely narrow definition of masculinity they were taught as boys.

What do you feel shame about?

How does your feeling of shame affect you and the choices you make in your life?

Do you feel like your shame stops you from moving forward or living fully?

If you are already in the process of healing from shame, what strategies have worked for you? Do you ever feel shame returning? How does it show up for you?

Day 15

*"If your compassion doesn't include yourself,
it is incomplete."*

—JACK KORNFIELD

Early in our 40-day adventure, I "outed" the inner critic as the great saboteur of your future, brilliant creations (not to mention the eroder of your self-esteem and the derailer of all enjoyment in life!) and shared a few things I've learned about this internal voice.

Today, I'd like to take a step sideways and feel for something kinder.

There is a softer, quieter presence within us that is available; we just have to be willing to reach for it. I first encountered this presence in a workshop setting, during a writing exercise offered by the facilitator.

She asked us to think of a situation we were struggling with and had us jot down a few lines about the situation at the top of a piece of paper.

For instance, *I'm not happy in my job, but I'm afraid to leave it and try to find something else* or *I find it really hard to set boundaries with my teenager even though they are disrespectful and mean.*

Then, we drew a vertical line down the middle of the page and labelled the left-hand column "Inner Critic" and the right-hand column "Inner Friend." The facilitator instructed us to write from the perspective of each of these voices that we carry within us when considering the situation we had outlined at the top.

My critic's voice came through immediately and loudly. I didn't have to strain to hear it at all! My left-hand list was packed with short, sharp bullet points of black and white statements and mocking questions. *What is wrong with you? You're never going to get anywhere. Why don't you quit now and stop making a fool of yourself?*

When I turned my attention to the other side of the page, the first thing I heard was a deafening silence. I took a deep breath, as the facilitator had suggested, and listened in again. Suddenly, I found myself writing the words *Dear Renée*. What followed was a stunningly beautiful letter that made me cry. It was full of warm and gentle support but also wisdom. In contrast to the spirit-breaking criticism on the other side, my inner friend calmed me, grounded me, and encouraged me.

This profound experience reminded me of the peace and presence I had discovered on the park bench in my 10 minutes of quiet. Only now, there were words to accompany the warm and peaceful feeling. I likened it to changing the dial on a radio station. I didn't have to listen to Critic FM all day, every day. I had a choice! And so do you.

We have a choice because this gentleness, kindness, and support is what we use every day with the people we love. It lives within us. It's the gift we give to others, but sadly, it's not how we usually treat ourselves.

You can name this other perspective whatever most resonates with you. The inner friend. Your inside champion. Call it whatever you like, but make sure to try and find it within you. It can remind you that you are a good person, trying hard and doing your best.

Connecting with this kind and friendly perspective inside of us is another tool we can use, like the appreciation practice I wrote about on Day 13. It's one we can offer ourselves when our critic is shouting or fear is blocking the way.

YOUR WRITING

The critic is loud and used to ruling the roost, so be patient with yourself. If this is the first time you are trying to "change the channel," make sure to take lots of deep breaths and really listen for something kinder within you.

Do the same exercise I wrote about, taking a thorny issue from your own life. Give yourself two columns, one for your inner critic and one for your inner friend, and write from each perspective. After you've done that, consider these questions:

What was it like to consult both voices about something important? Write about your experience. What did you learn?

What might help you to lower the volume of the critic?

How can you remember to change the channel and hear the perspective of your inner friend?

Write about some ways you might be able to tap into this kinder perspective more often.

Day 16

*"Instructions for living a life: Pay attention.
Be astonished. Tell about it."*

—MARY OLIVER

A few years ago, I participated in a month-long Poetry Challenge. When I told some friends about it, there was ample commentary and also some confusion.

One of them assumed I would be *reading* one poem a day. Poems that someone else had written. "What a nice idea," she said. Then I told her I was the one *writing* the poems. I could see an incredulous "Why?" forming behind her eyes. Another friend exclaimed, "I didn't think you wrote poetry!" And yet another sighed deeply and said, "That sounds just awful." Poetry gets such a bad rap, doesn't it?

For me, it wasn't about the act of writing poetry at all. It was about noticing what was right in front of me and choosing to pay close attention. Close enough that I could write a poem about a moment or an experience or a feeling of my choosing.

Having to write a poem a day woke me up to what is always right there. For me, it was a way to slow down and see differently. When we stop and pay attention to the shape of a cloud or the way the song sparrow's beak lifts as it sings or the light in our child's hair or the flecks of gold in our lover's eyes, we are opening to the magic that is always there but that we often miss.

Establishing a practice like this also really helps us to pinpoint what touches or moves us. It helps us to be a little more present to the richness that each day holds. When we pay attention, there are so many moments that have the potential to be a poem or a gorgeous piece of music or a beautiful painting or a should-be-framed photo.

A photographer friend of mine who also did the Poetry Challenge said this: "I realize that with my camera, I am not 'capturing' something. I am kissing it, communing with it, honouring it. It feels the same when I write a poem each day."

I love this idea of honouring at least some of our many moments here on Earth. There is something very special that happens when we open to a moment and allow ourselves a deep dive. It feels sacred.

YOUR WRITING

Today, I'd like you to kiss a moment of your choosing and write a poem about it. This doesn't have to be a moment from today. Feel free to use a moment from a special time, no matter how long ago.

Afterwards, I'd like you to spend a few minutes writing about why you chose the moment you did and what impact writing a poem about it had on you.

If you're not used to writing poetry, how did it feel to write a poem?

Write about other ways you might like to explore "kissing the moment." Photographs? Paintings? Sketches? Songs?

Day 17

"Playfulness is, in part, an openness to being a fool, which is a combination of not worrying about competence, not being self-important, not taking norms as sacred and finding ambiguity and double edges a source of wisdom and delight."

—MARIA LUGONES

I'd like to ask you to reread the quote above and really let it sink in. Being willing to be a fool. How many adults do you know who embrace this as their modus operandi? Likely not many. The strong and clear message we receive as we grow up is that we must be serious and responsible. We must be good at our jobs. We must make enough money. We must pay our taxes. We must take care of everyone who is relying on us.

For women especially, these messages cause us to learn the art of "master juggling"—parcelling out time dedicated to children, to chores, to meals, to work, to bills. We encourage our children to "go out and play," while we check things off our endless to-do lists. There is not much fun to be had.

Think back to when you were a kid. Do you remember how you used to play? How you made stuff up constantly? The imaginative games that felt so real? That "make-believe" mindset is still available to us as adults and, if accessed, helps us reclaim parts of ourselves that were lost as we became serious, practical, grown-up people.

What if I told you that figuring out a way to "play" as an adult would decrease your stress levels and increase creativity, happiness, and productivity? It's true! There's research that proves it.

Play allows us to be in the moment again, like we were when we were kids. More focused on what we are experiencing or creating than on the outcome or the result. This might mean going for a walk or a bike ride, not to get anywhere and not for exercise, but for the sheer enjoyment of it. Or the next time you take your kids to the arcade or the playground or the science museum, you could join in, rather than watching them.

Fred Rogers, whom you probably know as Mister Rogers, would sometimes sit down at a little table on the set of his TV show and draw something that was part of the story he was

DAY 17

telling. He'd show the picture and say something like: "I'm not very good at it, but it doesn't matter. It feels good to have made something."

Being willing to fail and being willing to be seen as a fool might just free you. Today, reach out and touch that childlike sense of wonder again. Relearn how to feel loose and light and free.

YOUR WRITING

Today's playful activity has three playful parts!

Part One:
Begin writing, one word following the next, choosing any words you want, but they must be in alphabetical order. Your words can either string together to make sense as a sentence or not. For example:

A big crusty diaper escaped from Giovanni's handbag…(etc.)

OR

Almond baguette crunch date efficiency flipper goddess horse….(etc.)

Do this two or three times in a row, going all the way through the alphabet each time, allowing yourself the joy of just playing with words.

Part Two:
Write a brief reflection on the role of "play" in your life.

What were your favourite forms of play as a child?

What do you do for play as an adult?

Do you make "play" a priority, or does it take a back seat in your life? Whatever your answer is, explain it.

When are you at your most playful? Are there new types of play you would like to try?

Part Three:
Do something playful today. Choose something from your list above—something you used to do or something you'd like to try—and do it!

Day 18

*"The only way through pain is to absorb,
probe, understand exactly what it is and
what it means. To close the door
on pain is to miss the chance for growth."*

—MAY SARTON

In addition to being a time of carefree play, childhood can also be the setting for our biggest wounds. Wounds that may remain unhealed and still have an impact. Other children can be cruel, and parents or teachers can be unthinking. If we have been criticized as children and that criticism was levelled at anything creative or artistic about us, it likely had the effect of stopping us from ever attempting that particular activity again.

Maybe you came home in tears with a story you'd been proud of, now sullied with red pen and a big fat D. Or perhaps the music teacher let the other kids sing out but told you to mouth the words. Maybe you thought your ceramic flower vase was beautiful and you couldn't wait to give it to your mom, but your older brother fell on the floor in a fit of hysterics when he saw it.

When we're children, we haven't yet developed the kind of protection we do later in life. We don't have the thick skin or the shields that we later use. We can't reason or argue with what a parent or a teacher or an older sibling says. We don't have the resources yet to be able to tell ourselves a different story: "They don't know what they're talking about," or "They're just being mean," or "They've got their own issues with creativity."

If someone tells you that your art sucks when you're a kid, it will have an impact. Art is a unique expression of who you are, so when someone tells you: "Your art is no good," it feels as if they're really saying: "You're no good." And these deep wounds of childhood criticism can affect us right into adulthood.

Our urge to create is our life force, so when we are kids and someone tries to snuff out our little creative lights (inadvertently or not), we end up with a little less life thrumming through us.

DAY 18

The amazing thing, though, is that this creative light inside of us still wants to shine. Despite the criticism. Despite the wounds. And this light continues to call to us from the inside. It wants to be let it out. I believe it does this until the day we die.

Today, I want to assure you that it's still possible to heal and shine. And there are things you can do that will help you reclaim and build your creative power. One of these is to write your story.

YOUR WRITING

Today, we are going to reflect on a scarring incident from the past. Choose one that you think impacted either your ability to be creative or your confidence, take a few deep breaths, and then pick from the options below:

Option One:
Write the story of this incident but from another perspective: someone else who was there, the cat on the sill, or even a spider in her corner web.

Option Two:
Write the story of this incident from your own perspective

but change the details of the story so that it has a different and more empowering ending.

Option Three:
Write a letter to the person at the heart of this incident, explaining what they did and how it impacted you. Make sure to give yourself closure on this. Perhaps tell them that you're choosing to move on from this experience now and that their critical words or actions have stopped you for long enough. (You don't have to send this letter.)

Be kind to yourself as you write today. These memories can be difficult and painful.

Day 19

"Steal from anywhere that resonates with inspiration or fuels your imagination. Devour old films, new films, music, books, paintings, photographs, poems, dreams, random conversations, architecture, bridges, street signs, trees, clouds, bodies of water, light, and shadows. Select only things to steal from that speak directly to your soul."

—JIM JARMUSCH

I love this quote, although I'm not crazy about the word "steal." Is it stealing to appreciate and be inspired by another human being's creation? Is it stealing to enjoy a pink sky in the morning or birds flying overhead, their wings glinting silver in the sunlight?

I don't think so. But Jarmusch isn't alone in his assessment of art as theft. In his book *Steal Like an Artist*, the author Austin Kleon argues that all art has been done before and "nothing is original." When I first read this, I thought this notion was offensive and nearly put the book down. I'm glad I didn't, because I learned that what Kleon is actually saying is that human beings are constantly improving on what others have done before them. We're always building on what's already been created. Nothing comes into being from nothing.

Kleon himself has portraits of favourite artists on the walls of his studio to inspire him. He says that seeing himself as part of a creative lineage helps him feel less alone. "They're like friendly ghosts. I can almost feel them pushing me forward as I'm hunched over my desk."

Kleon advises budding artists to choose their own friendly ghost—a favourite thinker, writer, or artist—and really study them. Investigate everything they created, and hone in on what you love about them. And then begin to copy them.

I remember doing this quite unconsciously in high school with the poetry of e.e. cummings. Something about the way he played with words, and the sentiments he evoked, really spoke to me. When I look back now, I can see I was copying his style, and I can also see how that led to me to finding more of my own voice later on.

YOUR WRITING

I'd like you to have a look at some of the things that "speak directly to your soul." We're going to see if we can harness their power to create something fresh and original, something that might even be surprising.

Taking time to notice and respond to what moves us is a vital part of self-reflection. Honouring what has an impact on us can be a door to knowing ourselves in a deeper, more soulful way.

Write down the following on a piece of paper (you are going to cut this piece of paper up, so make sure it's not in your journal!):

- a lyric from one of your all-time favourite songs (maybe the one you always shout out when you're singing along, or the one that moves you to tears)
- a line from a cherished poem
- a favourite quote or saying; this could also be a blessing or a prayer
- finally, try to call up the last compliment someone gave you and use the person's exact words if you can remember them

Take a pair of scissors and cut out each word from all of these lines above. For instance, if your song lyric was "Don't stop believing," the words "don't" and "stop" and "believing" would end up being three different pieces of paper.

Now, shuffle all your pieces of paper and lay them out on a table. Have a look at all these different words and see which ones jump out at you, or which ones go together (ones that weren't together initially).

What can you create with these words that were once someone else's? Does a story idea pop out? Or perhaps a first line of a poem? Use this exercise as inspiration, and then run with it and create something that is unique to you.

Have fun!

Day 20

"Our consciousness rarely registers the beginning of a growth within us any more than without us: there have been many circulations of the sap before we detect the smallest sign of the bud."

—MARY ANN EVANS (George Eliot)

One day, a number of years ago, my partner and I were walking in a large urban park near our home. It was early on a Sunday and mostly quiet. We reached a "fork in the roads" place, where a number of different paths converged, and were astonished to discover quite a substantial group of people milling about.

It appeared to be a big club of weekend runners who had

stopped to take a break mingling with what looked like a large pack of dog-walkers. Dogs and people were everywhere, and because our walk had been quiet up to then, the bustling energy of all these beings took us by surprise.

"A crowd in the forest!" my partner exclaimed as we waded through the smell of coffee and the sound of laughter and tried not to trip over the dogs underfoot.

This description—*a crowd in the forest*—stuck. We now use it to describe any experience we have where we're totally taken by surprise. Where, suddenly, life veers off script. This could be anything that takes you out of a relatively peaceful, ordinary existence and thrusts you into something else entirely. I think of Covid as a universal crowd in the forest.

My hope is that there have been no "crowd in the forest" moments for you during the first 20 days on your path. Crowds in the forest can throw us off our game and toss new routines completely out the window. If something *has* happened—your cat got sick, your mom broke her hip, your teenager needed you to edit a massive research assignment—don't be hard on yourself for missing a few days.

Just start again. Always start again.

Even if life hasn't thrown you a curveball, three weeks of a new practice can be a time when the rubber meets the road. Remember the oft-quoted theory that it takes 21 days to form a new habit? That idea has since been labelled a myth. Researchers now say that it can take up to eight months to create and sustain new behaviours, and not all of those days are going to feel incredible. Some days will be neutral, others will be a grind.

Recall the "slack workout" from Day 9—keep going, even if you're not feeling it. Put the effort in, take kind note of all you've accomplished so far, and remind yourself of the reasons you're doing this.

Halfway through a 40-day process is a significant milestone. It means you've been getting really good at offering yourself the gift of time, space, and hopefully, kindness. Give yourself a high five! And keep going!

YOUR WRITING

Some questions to reflect on as you ease your way over the halfway mark:

What have you noticed since you started this work? Are there subtle shifts and changes that you're aware of? These can be internal or more tangible. Write them down, even if they feel vague.

Reread the George Eliot quote at the top. What is beginning to grow in you but is not yet a leaf or a flower or even a bud? What is the sap that is running in you but is not yet tapped?

Day 21

*"Ideas are like rabbits.
You get a couple, learn how to handle them,
and pretty soon you have a dozen."*

—JOHN STEINBECK

Whether you are in touch with your natural creativity and routinely tapping into it or whether you feel you are gently coming back into contact with this part of you, ideas are the seeds from which everything grows. They are central to the business of being creative.

As such, they must be respected, honoured, and tended.

How do you respect an idea? By writing it down. By visiting it. By thinking about it.

How do you honour an idea? By acknowledging that it might one day be something that takes physical form and becomes a part of here-and-now reality.

How do you tend an idea? By recognizing it is a gift from a friendly universe that is using ideas to connect and communicate with you.

How do you know an idea is good? Sometimes there is a feeling that comes with an idea, either goosebumps or a sense of rightness. Some people talk about an idea that wouldn't let them go. Other people talk about the good idea that got away—someone else ended up writing that book or making that film.

In her book *Big Magic*, Elizabeth Gilbert writes about how she believes that ideas are a life-form with an energy and a consciousness all their own. And she says that this consciousness has one desire: To be created. To be made real. Gilbert believes that ideas "spend eternity swirling around us, searching for available and willing human partners."

These are not just artistic ideas, but scientific and commercial and political ideas as well. And when they find a suitable and willing human, one who actually pays attention, the idea will first send what Gilbert calls "universal physical and emotional signals of inspiration"—chills up the arms, hair standing up on the back of the neck—followed by serendipities that feel like signs and keep your interest keen.

DAY 21

Whether or not you believe the intriguing notion that ideas are alive and seeking you out, it's worth spending some time mulling over your own ideas. I find that the more I write my ideas down, the more come. Some of them remain incomprehensible notes to myself on a scrap of paper that I find years later. Others become something. What's the difference? I'm not sure. Ideas are mysterious, just like us.

YOUR WRITING

Today, I want you to begin to think about your ideas and to connect with your own mysterious process. Some questions to guide you:

Make a list of really good ideas you had that became a reality. Do you remember how the ideas came to you? Do you remember how you went about making these ideas live and breathe?

How do you know if something is a good idea? Do you have any physical sensations? Or a gut feeling? Something else?

When do you have your best ideas? Have you ever wondered why ideas come to you then?

Write about how you honour and tend your ideas. And if you don't currently do that, write about how you wish or plan to be more respectful of these gifts.

Day 22

*"Bravery isn't about being fearless.
It's about loyalty, loyalty to yourself."*

—LIGHT WATKINS

On Day 11, I wrote about the soul voice—the part of us that knows our truth and will speak it, whether or not we're ready to listen. But how many of us act in accordance with this voice? Are we respecting the wisdom that it offers? Are we consulting it when we make decisions?

Or are we ignoring it and plunging forward, making choices based on external factors like what other people think and what our parents want and what careers pay the best?

For years, I let my soul voice speak, but only in my journal. I would write about the stuff I hoped for, ideas I had, things I wanted for my life. I found one of these journals recently and here's what I read: "I have so many dreams, but I don't feel good enough for any of them."

I feel heartsick for this young person who felt unworthy of her deepest, most heartfelt desires, but it's easy to see now that this feeling of unworthiness was directly connected to the shame I wrote about on Day 14. I felt shame about who I was, so it's no wonder that I didn't feel worthy of the things I dreamed about—being a writer, finding love, living a joyful life.

In her book *Radical Acceptance*, psychologist and Buddhist teacher Tara Brach calls this "the trance of unworthiness." She says that this "experience of personal deficiency is a pervasive form of suffering, with its roots in societal norms that assign superior value to certain races, types of intelligence, appearance, sexual orientation, behaviour, and performance." She also says that for many of us these feelings of deficiency are easily triggered. "It doesn't take much—just hearing of someone else's accomplishments, being criticized, getting into an argument, making a mistake at work—to make us feel that we are not okay."

When I look back now, I can clearly see the connection between how I felt about myself and the choices I ended up making. I didn't feel worthy of what was calling me from within, so how could I even begin taking steps in the direction of my innermost desires and dreams?

DAY 22

This led to a series of random decisions: taking jobs that were offered to me or that other people thought I'd be good at, getting the education I thought my parents wanted, staying in relationships despite misgivings, and helping other people fulfill their dreams while mine stayed locked in the pages of my journal.

Beginning to feel worthy of my own inner callings has taken years of therapy, a mid-life wake-up call, and a lot of soulful introspection. I can't give you a recipe, but I can give you two absolutely essential ingredients: compassion and kindness. I had to teach myself to see my whole life—including my own feelings of shame and unworthiness and all the associated missteps—through a more compassionate lens. This is not a done deal. The work is ongoing.

YOUR WRITING

Today, with gentleness and compassion, begin to inquire into whether a sense of unworthiness is keeping you from listening and responding to any of your own inner callings. Here are some questions to guide you:

Did my story of feeling unworthy resonate with you? How does that feeling show up in your life?

Take an inventory of your inner hopes or dreams. Are there any that elicit a feeling of not being good enough? Do you doubt that you deserve to bring them alive? Explore and shed light on this through your writing.

Day 23

"Our job in this life is not to shape ourselves into some ideal we imagine we ought to be, but to find out who we already are and become it."

—STEVEN PRESSFIELD

That sense of unworthiness I wrote about yesterday permeated many of my major life decisions and caused me to take more than one job that wasn't aligned with my inner being. One of these was a full-time job I had in my late twenties. The salary and benefits were good, and I was working alongside people who had made this work their career. But I was miserable.

I remember moments of rising panic, sitting in my office and looking out at the world. I watched people walk by, imagining they had their lives figured out and wondering what was wrong with me, because I was nearly 30 in a job I didn't like with no idea how to do anything differently.

And then one day, I saw a flyer at the library. And then I saw it again at the café. And again at the bookstore. *Women and Writing Workshop*, it said: an eight-week session for women to explore themselves and their lives through writing.

Every time I saw that flyer, I knew it was for me. There was a quiet and tender and excited YES inside of me. Don't get me wrong, I was terrified. I remember shaking like a leaf when I introduced myself on the first night. But I also remember the feeling of closeness that grew among the women in the group.

There was tea and there were tears and there was laughter and there was the sound of our pens scratching on paper, and then our voices reading our words aloud. The facilitator would recite poems and tell us about books she loved and ask us deep and meaningful questions.

The writing I did and the sharing within the group quickly became the highlight of my week. I felt like myself in this group, or more accurately, that the group was helping me *become* myself. And this was a very different feeling than the one I had when I sat in my office, feeling empty and wondering what the hell I was doing.

When I look back from my current vantage point, it's easy to see why I was so drawn to the writing group. It offered me an early experience of what I would become. A precursor. A premonition. A signpost. A breadcrumb on my path. That group embodied everything that I have since created for myself—a life spent writing, a life surrounded by words and books, a life where I connect deeply with other writers.

YOUR WRITING

Have you had the kind of experience I've just described? When something feels so right? When it just feels like YOU? And when you look back on it later, you can see how that knowing led to something extraordinarily beautiful?

What is your "becoming" story?

And if you feel like you are still on your way there, what do you long to become? Are there signposts or breadcrumbs on your path? Describe them.

Are there things you are resisting now that would help in your becoming process? Explore this in your writing.

Day 24

*"I became a writer out of desperation....
When I was young, younger than I am now,
I started to write about my own life and
I came to see that this act saved my life."*

—JAMAICA KINCAID

In her book *How to Stay Sane*, British therapist Philippa Perry names "self-observation" as a cornerstone of mental health. She says that the continuing development of "a non-judgmental, observing part of ourselves is crucial for our wisdom and sanity."

I absolutely believe this to be true and discovered it first-hand with the other women in the weekly writing group I wrote about yesterday. We explored our lives and our hearts through the questions posed by the facilitator. She asked us what we most longed for. She inquired about our greatest secrets and our biggest shames. She dared us to take off the mask we show the world and to risk being vulnerable and true.

My handwriting changed throughout the course—from clenched and tentative to free-flowing, the pages dense with words. When I hold the notebook in my hands now, decades later, I can feel how hard I was pressing. Life began to flow from me in words on the page, freeing something knotted inside.

It was a powerful and meaningful time. I learned to listen and acknowledge my inner self and begin to care for her. It's also where I came to understand that our lives can be transformed through honest self-reflection. If we have the courage to look at our most difficult or traumatic experiences, writing about them helps to shine a light on something that has often been hidden. Writing gives us a safe space to examine these painful things and work on them.

And it's during this examination of our emotional wounds or traumas that flashes of insight or shifts in perspective can occur. We might suddenly achieve an awareness that we didn't have prior to writing, one that changes our relationship to ourselves and to others.

In her incredible book *Writing as a Way of Healing: How*

DAY 24

Telling Our Stories Transforms Our Lives, Louise DeSalvo tells about the "health and emotional benefits of opening up through writing."

She cites a research study that found that people who wrote detailed accounts of traumatic events in their lives, which included *their feelings* about what happened, had improved health and a sense of well-being.

She says this: "Writing that describes traumatic or distressing events in detail *and* how we felt about these events then and how we feel about them now is the only kind of writing about trauma that clinically has been associated with improved health. Simply writing about innocuous subjects or simply writing about traumatic events or venting our feeling about trauma without *linking* the two does not result in significant health or emotional benefits."

Although powerful, this kind of writing can also be scary and intense. It's important, if you are drawn to writing as a form of healing, that you have some good supports, perhaps in the form of a therapist or a close friend or a support group. There are also some good books out there that can help to guide your process. One is DeSalvo's book, and another is *Writing for Your Life: A Guide and Companion to the Inner Worlds*, by Deena Metzger.

YOUR WRITING

You may or may not be ready for what Louise DeSalvo recommends. Check in with yourself and choose between these two options for today's writing:

- Do as DeSalvo advises above: Choose a traumatic experience. Write about it in detail. Make sure to include how you felt about it—then and now.

OR

- Write about your life as a fairy tale. Your story can be as long or short as you would like. Include some or all of the traditional elements. You, of course, are the hero. Is there a villain? Is there a journey? Are there magical elements? Talking animals? A witch? A wizard? A guide?

Begin with "Once upon a time..." and write it in the third person (e.g., she, they, he). This gives you the opportunity to step back, observe your life, and have the distance to really explore your challenges, your strengths, and your victories.

Day 25

"The most regretful people on earth are those who felt the call to creative work, who felt their own creative power restive and uprising, and gave to it neither power nor time."

—MARY OLIVER

So, what happens if you know, without a shadow of a doubt, what your soul voice wants? And you agree that you should a) write that book, b) make that movie, c) go on that trip, d) leave your relationship, e) quit your job, f) start your own business, g) go back to school, but you just can't figure out how to fulfill this calling of your soul?

Maybe you quit before you start or you stop halfway through. Maybe you believe, like I did, that your big dream is too big or that you're not good enough or skilled enough to bring it alive. Maybe it all feels impossible and terrifying and too much.

First of all, you're not alone. No one approaches a big, soulful desire without trepidation and insecurity and fear. Second, there's a name for this phenomenon. It's a nice big inclusive word that author Steven Pressfield uses in his book *The War of Art*, which I highly recommend. It's called Resistance. With a capital R.

"Most of us have two lives," he writes. "The life we live and the unlived life within us. Between the two stands Resistance." Pressfield calls Resistance "the most toxic force on the planet" and believes that this force not only stunts our growth, but mars and deforms our spirit. That's serious stuff.

If you want to write a book but you can't seem get to your desk, that's Resistance. If you want to get in shape but you don't get off the couch. If you want to act, but you watch movies instead. If you want to start a business. If you want to stop drinking. If you want to take a stand.

At the root of all the failed attempts and all the procrastination is Resistance, which seems to exist to push us away from our most deeply held desires.

What's a human to do?

Remember that co-operative and powerful universal force that I wrote about on Day 10? The one some people call God, and others call the Divine or spiritual electricity or the Universe? Pressfield believes in this energy too. And he says we can actively enlist the support of what he calls "angels" and "muses" in overcoming Resistance. The secret is in doing the work, in simply starting.

"When we sit down each day and do our work, power concentrates around us. The Muse takes note of our dedication. She approves.... When we sit down and work, we become like a magnetized rod that attracts iron filings. Ideas come. Insights accrete."

The War of Art changed my life and gave me courage. What a relief to find out that I wasn't the only one procrastinating on my dreams. There wasn't anything wrong with me; I was battling against the same force we all do. And it doesn't have to win, this negative force of Resistance. There is a way through.

YOUR WRITING

Let's explore the unique way that Resistance shows up in your life. A few questions to get you started:

What do you think of this concept of Resistance? Is it new to you? Does it resonate with your experience?

How does Resistance manifest for you? Procrastination? Video game compulsion? Aimless phone scrolling?

What is the impact of Resistance in your life? What is it keeping you from?

What do you think of the idea of using "angels" and "muses" to help you tackle Resistance and more fully become who you are?

And if you don't believe in the existence of friendly helpers, can you come up with other suggestions that might work to help you "resist" Resistance?

Day 26

"I did not lose myself all at once. I rubbed out my face over the years washing away my pain, the same way carvings on stone are worn down by water."

—AMY TAN

I have a rum and coke in my hands. The glass is sweating. I feel too shy to move off the couch. I suddenly realize that my lips have gone completely numb. This has never happened with a glass of wine at home with my parents.

I feel like everyone is staring at me, and I'm sure it's because I don't belong at this party. "What is she doing here?" I imagine them saying. I had been surprised to get an invite at all, but also delighted and terribly nervous. I had spent a long time on my hair and picking the right sweater. And now I have to pee.

It takes a while for me to work up the courage to get off the couch, and when I do, the floor seems to tip a bit like I'm on a boat. I look at myself in the bathroom mirror and see glassy eyes and flushed cheeks. I feel better standing and my stomach does an excited little leap to actually be at a high school party, something I'd longed for. There's a little group gathered outside the bathroom door, and the party host grabs my glass and refills it.

As I stand and sip, there is a feeling settling over me—of comfort and ease. I even feel free enough to add something to the conversation, and what I say makes people laugh. I see a few of them shoot me a look, and there's something new there, something like respect or surprise in their eyes. And then someone grabs my arm while they are telling a story and someone else bumps hips with me. I feel an opening. As if these social doors, long closed to me, are finally unlocked, and all I had to do was push on them and then slide inside.

My lips are still numb and I'm aware that the walls are leaning in on me, but it isn't an aggressive, unfriendly leaning. It is a conspiratorial, warm leaning that matches this spacious new feeling of belonging.

♥

DAY 26

That was 17-year-old me, learning early that alcohol was some kind of magic elixir that made me feel better about myself. When I drank, I was less shy and more brave. When I drank, I fit in. And when I drank, I didn't feel as bad about who I was—a lesbian in a teenaged girl's body—in a high school and a city and a culture and a time where being gay was very, very wrong.

After this first party experience, alcohol became my crutch and remained so for the next 33 years. I don't resonate with the terms "addicted" or "alcoholic," so I don't use them. I know what it was about for me and why I had to stop. I used it to feel better about myself and to soothe a private, internal sense of shame, all the while telling myself lies about why I drank. To have fun. To take the edge off. To relax. To unwind. Really, it was to feel more normal and to somehow anchor and support the sensitive, hurting child who felt her very essence was deeply wrong and unlovable.

At the root of all of our crutches, I believe, is a feeling of not being good enough. It is one of shame. And we look to something outside of us to make it better. To make us feel better or at least less screwed up. For some people, it's over-working or over-giving. For others it's TV or shopping or sex. For still others, it might be cigarettes or gambling or drugs or technology.

Whatever it is for you, it's important to recognize that your crutch (or crutches—we often have more than one!) does not define you.

YOUR WRITING

Sometimes we want to remain in happy oblivion about our crutches. Turning toward them with a magnifying glass might feel scary or dangerous. Try to cultivate a spirit of curiosity when responding to these writing prompts.

Do you feel you have a crutch? Describe what it is and how you use it.

If there is more than one, note them all, but choose one to go deeper with in this piece of writing. Be as honest as you can. You're the only one who is going to read this.

What is at the root of your crutch? Why do you use it? When did it start and how has it evolved? What does the crutch do for you? Are there things your crutch is keeping you from?

Can you see a life without your crutch? Can you make out any first tentative steps to get there?

Day 27

"When a person can't find a deep sense of meaning, they distract themselves with pleasure."

—VIKTOR FRANKL

If you google the words "screen time," many of the first results you'll see are about how adults should be controlling or limiting how much time their children spend in front of their devices. But what about us adults? We seem to recognize the importance of *children* being encouraged to go outside, read books, play, and be active, but somehow this logic doesn't apply to us in the same way.

So many of us are on our computers or our phones all day for work. And then we reward ourselves with a little "downtime" on Instagram or Netflix or our favourite games app, rather than being active, reading a book, or going for a walk. Our phones, especially, are such an easy "treat." They are usually close by, they are always ON, and they house an endless supply of compelling and distracting information.

If you grew up in the '70s and '80s like I did, the idea of carrying a telephone that also contains books, games, music, and vast swaths of information is kind of crazy. When I was growing up, the phone was attached to the wall, books were at the library, music was on the radio or the record player, the games were in the cupboard, and encyclopedias were where all the knowledge was stored. Times have changed!

While these tiny powerful computers we carry around with us are absolutely impressive, they are also enormous time-suckers. Internet content is *designed* to keep us scrolling, keep us clicking, keep us engaged and consuming. It's hard to resist! We don't even notice how much time is passing when we are aimlessly scrolling.

It takes intent and stamina to not constantly give in to this draw. If these 40 days are revealing to you that there is something unique you want to create, but you find yourself distracted by technology, you might want to consider forming some boundaries.

Here are a few tips from my own experience:

- Consider silencing your computer and phone while you

are doing any creative work. Not hearing the beeping or humming notifications helps with focus.

- If you love word games but tend to get sucked down the slippery rabbit hole of the apps on your phone, what about going old school? Crossword puzzle books where you work with a nice sharp pencil. Or Scrabble or Boggle or Bananagrams. And don't forget to delete the word game apps on your phone. Not having them right there at your fingertips will help a lot.

- If you want to reduce your screen time, use the settings on your device to keep track and set daily time limits for yourself. The reminder that pops up when your time is over will help you keep your promises to yourself.

- Consider going on a "technology cleanse," where you put away all devices for a day or more at a time.

If your screen time is keeping you from living fully, connecting with others, or moving toward a creative dream, simply becoming aware of how often you are on a screen can be a first step in reclaiming some of your precious time and energy.

YOUR WRITING

In the days ahead, try to notice how often you are using technology, what you are using it for, and how it makes you feel. Some questions to guide your writing today:

Write about when and how you use technology.

How do you feel about how often you are on screens?

Are there changes you want to make in your relationship with technology? Write them down and be specific.

Is there something non-screen-related that would help bring more balance?

Is there anything your screen time is keeping you from? What might be possible without it?

Day 28

"To be ourselves causes us to be exiled by many others, and yet to comply with what others want causes us to be exiled from ourselves."

—CLARISSA PINKOLA ESTÉS

How many times a day do you stop yourself from doing or saying something because you're afraid of what someone else will think? If you take this question seriously and start noticing, I would bet money that you'd lose count before the day is done.

Don't be too upset. You're in good company. I believe that most of us, unless you were raised by super-enlightened parents (or wolves), have been trained to care deeply about what other people think.

In fact, research shows that, like the negativity bias I wrote about on Day 13, this fixation on what other people think of us is a product of human evolution. In the distant past, when humans were dependent on their community for everything, it was important to stay in good standing. If you did something that got you kicked out of the tribe, you were as good as dead.

In that context, what other people thought was extremely important. Now, not so much. That isn't to say that you should go around treating people like crap and not caring. But some of us care a bit too much, and we allow other people's judgments and opinions to affect our self-esteem or get in the way of what we actually want.

I remember when I first stopped drinking, I was nervous about what all my friends would think. Most of the people I hung out with at the time drank too, and the things we did together centred around drinking. If I had to pinpoint the exact fear I had, it was this: "They probably think I'm no fun anymore." This fear kept me from hanging out with them.

I ended up seeing my friends individually for a while—going for walks, going out for coffee, seeing a movie—and this helped. One day, quite early on, I met a friend at a café and she came right out and asked me the dreaded question, the one I'd feared! "So, are you any fun anymore?"

She laughed, obviously intending this as a joke, but it stung. It also solidified what I thought everyone was thinking.

Fast forward a few years and this same friend also gave up alcohol. She later fessed up to the rude question. "That was my stuff," she said. "I was afraid if I ever quit drinking, people would think *I* was no fun anymore."

This admission healed that moment in time for me, but it also taught me that other people's opinions are coloured by everything they've been through or are currently grappling with.

Something else to consider: We can't control what other people think, but more than that, we can never truly *know* what someone else is thinking. What if our fear of "what other people think" is actually our own inner critic having a field day? We put words and feelings in other people's mouths and then use them to slay ourselves. And then we make important life decisions based on what our critic imagines these other people are thinking or saying about us.

Talk about a crazy-making situation!

YOUR WRITING

Today, I encourage you to really dig into this topic of how other people's thoughts, opinions, and judgments influence you. It's a large and complex one, but it's also capable of yielding some real gems, if you're willing to go deep.

Where does "fear of what others think" appear in your life? Does it interfere with your own well-being or self-esteem? Does it interfere with your decision making?

What stories do you fear people are telling about you?

Have a good hard look at those stories. Is it possible you are simply parroting the words of your own inner critic?

Day 29

"I wish I could show you, when you are lonely or in darkness, the astonishing light of your own being."

—HAFIZ

As I've already written, I had a habit of drinking to emotionally soothe myself. This went on for many years, and even though I would repeatedly come to the realization that I should stop, I never could. Until I did.

But I truly don't think I would have gotten there if it hadn't been for my partner. When I told her that I wanted to stop drinking, she was calm and unconcerned. "I'll stop with you," she said. "We won't drink together."

I was so grateful for this offer and also for the fact that she didn't appear ruffled or at all judgmental. We'd only been together one year at that point. It could have been a deal breaker, but instead she was only kind and supportive and has never gone back on her offer to not drink, which has helped me keep my promise to myself.

I tell you this story because I think it illustrates how with support, we are all able to do hard things.

I know someone who came out of an abusive relationship feeling isolated and desperate. She reached out to her oldest and dearest friends and asked for their help in reminding her who she was before the abuse. These friends sent her photos and memories and quotes and poems and songs until she gradually started to feel steady again. This daily contact reminded her who she still was. With the help of these friends, she was able to return to herself.

The list of examples of how we humans need each other is endless. We see it in the friend who goes to chemo with you. The friend who trains for the Camino with you. The friends who want to limit their time on social media and make a pact with each other. The group that writes together and gives each other feedback and praise.

Being accountable to someone else for the commitments you make can help take these promises to the next level.

We are not alone. It can feel that way sometimes, but it's possible, if we ask, to be truly held and buoyed by the people who love us. I need to repeat an important part of that sentence.

If we ask.

This is the thing that sometimes seems the hardest to do. We don't want to impose. We don't want to seem needy. We don't want to "put anyone out."

But here's the truth. We simply can't do it alone. We need each other. We humans play such a vital role in each other's lives, and there are so many ways we can support each other and be supported. It only takes time and a little bravery to reach out.

YOUR WRITING

Surrounding ourselves with those who see us, appreciate us, and adore us for exactly who we are is one of the kindest things we can do for ourselves. And asking for help from these special people is also one of the smartest.

Who do you trust the most? Who can you call upon for help?

Write about a time in your life when someone else helped you do a big thing.

Is there a commitment you want to make to yourself that you need help with? Write it down. Who will you ask to help keep you on track?

Taking this one step further, I'd like you to prep an email or letter, asking for the help you need. And then...send it!

Day 30

"If the only prayer you ever say in your entire life is thank you, it will be enough."

—MEISTER ECKHART

Our lives are long and if we really turn our minds to it, there are so many people to thank. The therapist who helped us turn a corner. The teacher who encouraged a talent we didn't know we had. The friends who asked us to be brave in the face of fear.

A few years ago, I found some old letters from a long-ago friend. Julia was someone I worked with in my early twenties. She was older than me, definitely wiser, and she took the time to connect with me in a really sincere way. She asked big questions and wanted deep conversations. Even after I moved away, she stayed in touch, writing letters that continued our exchange and also my sense of being seen. Looking at these letters decades later, it was clear that she had planted seeds in me, ones that only cracked the soil and grew later, after we were no longer in touch.

The day I found her letters, I googled her name and quickly had a phone number. Without stopping to think, I called her and was able to thank her for being someone who had really made a difference in my life. She was surprised and delighted to hear from me and so appreciated that I had reached out. I'm very glad I did. It would have been easy to read those letters and privately acknowledge the role she played. But there was something really special in closing the loop.

A few years after that, I had the reverse experience when my dear friend Stuart wrote me a letter, describing in great detail all the wonderful things he saw in me. His letter made me cry. I had no idea he thought many of the things he wrote down. The fact that it was spontaneous (not for any special occasion), beautifully handwritten, and filled not only with his time, but with his heart, have all stayed with me. This gift became even more special after Stuart suffered a long illness and died.

All of us need to be seen for who we are and what we bring into the world. And I don't think we tell each other enough. In fact, with our closest people, I think we fall into the trap of noticing what our partner or our children or our siblings or our parents aren't doing "right." (*Why can't he ever remember to clear his plate? Why is she not listening to me?*)

What if we focused our attention on what we really love and appreciate about those who most closely share our lives? When was the last time we sat any one of them down to thank them for being the beautiful soul they are? Things like: *I love how you always find the perfect gift. I love the way you tell stories. I love listening to you sing when you think you're alone. I love that I can find you in the store by listening for your whistling.*

There is so much meaning and power in these acts of gratitude. When we express the love that is in our hearts and we do so in a very specific way, the other person feels seen and valued. And isn't that what we all want?

YOUR WRITING

This is the only day where your writing isn't *just* for you. Today, you are going to write a surprise card or letter or postcard to someone who is special and important to you. This could be an old friend from university days, a colleague, or someone you live with and see every day.

Get really specific and tell this person exactly what you most appreciate about them. Tell them the world is a better place with them in it. Regale them with details of all the things you like and admire about them. Fill your letter with love. And don't forget to deliver it!

Turning back to your own pages or journal now, write about how it felt to send this letter off and what kind of impact writing this letter had on you.

Day 31

"It is nothing to die. It is frightening not to live."

—VICTOR HUGO

I find the idea of death—which is actually the *fact* of death—to be so clarifying.

One day, this will all go on without me. One day someone else will be sitting at a desk in this little building in our backyard, hearing the birds, feeling the sun on the side of their face like I am now. One day, this building, this yard, this house, this neighbourhood may not be here at all, long after I'm dead and our children are dead and their children and their children too.

We are here for an alarmingly short period of time. That fact can either freak you out or help you try to live differently, perhaps aligning your life to who you are and what is in your heart a little bit more.

"I wish I'd had the courage to live a life true to myself, not the life others expected of me." This is the primary and most frequent regret shared by the palliative care patients author Bronnie Ware worked with. She recorded these powerful messages in her beautiful book *The Top Five Regrets of the Dying* in the hope that it would inspire people still living to be true to themselves before it was too late.

What Ware found in talking to the dying was that many of them realized, too late, they had forfeited their own agency in their biggest life decisions. They took jobs, built careers, chose partners, and decided where and how to live based on external, societal, and economic pressures. They talked about how, even though they felt an urge to make changes and go after their dreams, they hadn't taken action because they were afraid of rocking the boat and disappointing their families. They were afraid their colleagues would judge them. They were afraid everyone would think them a fool.

How many times have you heard the sad tale of someone who hated their job and was counting down the days until retirement? They wanted to make sure they got their full pension so they just kept adding things to their bucket list. And then they died. Just a month after they retired. Their first trip was booked but they hadn't left yet. Their bag was packed and ready to go.

We have a limited period of time in these human bodies, and what I'm advocating through the course of this book isn't time management or efficiency. It's taking the time to figure out how you—the most inner and sacred you—want to be spending those precious moments.

YOUR WRITING

Today, consider whether you can allow the reality of your own death, which is in some ways your only certainty, to guide you. How can you let it direct your life to more of the living you want to do?

Here are some questions to mull over:

What will you miss when you die?

What are you afraid of regretting at the end of your life?

What are you hoping you'll be most proud of?

If you were diagnosed with a condition that gave you only a short time to live, are there things you would change? How would you live differently?

Day 32

"When one is a stranger to oneself, then one is estranged from others, too. If one is out of touch with oneself, then one cannot touch others. Only when one is connected to one's own core, is one connected to others."

—ANNE MORROW LINDBERGH

I once heard the singer-songwriter Glen Hansard being interviewed on the radio. He's quite a genuine and insightful person, so he said a lot of amazing things, but one line in particular had me running for a pen and paper.

"There is a responsibility if you're a musician, if you've been given this sacred gift of being able to make music on any level, then you should really be using it to inspire."

I agree with him. Our gifts are meant to be shared. And when we use our gifts to touch others, some pretty incredible things can happen.

A documentarian once asked the Dalai Lama, "What is the most important meditation we can do now?"

Here's his powerful answer: "Critical thinking, followed by action. Discern what your world is. Know the plot, the scenario of this human drama. And then figure out where your talents might fit in to make a better world."

Depending on where you are on your path of becoming, this might all feel like a little too much. On the other hand, hearing this advice might really inspire you.

Back to Glen Hansard for a minute. He's one of the only musicians I have ever heard talk openly about the concept of "writing from within" rather than writing for commercial success. He says that the songs that came from his heart are the ones that have gone on to become hits. The truth within the songs resonates with others, forms a connection, and makes a difference.

"I like to write songs that will have a place in people's lives," he says. Whether that's a song that someone shares with their friends, or one they listen to over and over while getting over a breakup, or one that someone chooses for a wedding or a funeral, Hansard likes to think that his songs have a use in other humans' lives.

I like this thought a lot. That the things we do that are connected to our gifts, to our essence, and to our hearts can have a powerful effect on other people and their lives—if we are brave enough to share them.

YOUR WRITING

I want you to imagine you are spinning out a thread from your heart. The thread is your gift to the world. Watch it wind and curl its way toward another heart, and another beyond that, and another.

What does this thread look like?

What does it have to say?

Who is it touching?

What impact could it have?

How far could it reach?

Day 33

"The difference between who you want to be and who you are is what you do."

—CHARLES DUHIGG

On Day 9, I wrote about the wisdom of creating habits rather than relying only on inspiration. It's a good thing then that we humans are habit-making machines! As soon as any action becomes repetitive, the brain, which is wired to save energy, starts automating this behaviour. In other words, the brain easily and quickly creates a habit.

That's why, once we learn how to drive, it's easy to listen to the radio, think complex thoughts, or have a conversation, while still driving a one-ton vehicle! The driving itself becomes automated and our brain is free to use its energy elsewhere. Kind of amazing when you think of it!

And it all starts with a pattern called a "habit loop." In *The Power of Habit*, author Charles Duhigg explains this three-part process. First there is a cue or a trigger that tells your brain to begin the automated behaviour. Then there is the behaviour itself. And then there is a reward, something our brain likes that will help it remember this "habit loop" in the future.

If our habit loops are healthy, the automation works to our benefit. Think of the training involved in any fitness goal. We create cues that might include setting an alarm, meeting a friend, or laying out our workout clothes before we go to sleep. The fitness behaviour ensues and ends with the reward, which might be an endorphin rush or the happy feeling we get when the pants that didn't fit us a month ago suddenly do.

Of course, there's also a downside to the fact that it's easy for us to make new habits. Reaching for a glass of wine when the "stress" cue is triggered. Smoking a cigarette when your body gives you the cue of anxiety. Buying and consuming a cheese croissant every time you walk by the bakery and smell the delicious croissant cue.

Over these last 33 days, you've set up a new habit for yourself: reading each day and writing in answer to the prompt I've provided. If you've done your reading and writing at the same time and in the same place every day, you've likely created a habit that feels firmly ingrained by now. I hope this experience has shown you that it is possible to create new and nurturing habits, ones that serve you.

And when you look more closely, you've actually done more than form a simple reading and writing habit. You've created a deeper habit than that. One where you show up for yourself, where you pay attention to what's going on inside you, and where you think deeply about what you want to create and share with the world. This is powerful stuff!

But what about the habits you came into this practice with? There is likely a raft of other patterned behaviours, ones that may not match what you have discovered while you've been reading this book and writing every day. These habits might keep you from pursuing the dreams and goals and ambitions that are rising to the top. That's what we're going to work with today.

YOUR WRITING

Exploring our own habits can be a fascinating practice. There are so many habitual things that we do without even thinking. Today, we want to bring more consciousness to the habits that make up our lives.

First off, think about a typical day. As you mentally run

through all the things you do in the course of a day, identify some daily habits or patterns of behaviour. Try to go beyond brushing your teeth and write them all down.

Which of these habits do you feel good about?

Which of these habits don't serve you? Why don't they serve you? Is there an impact on your physical or mental health? Is there an impact on other people? On your work? On your time?

Would you like to stop some of these habits that don't serve you? Be specific about what needs to change and why. Also write about how you might attempt to make these needed changes.

Are there any new habits you feel drawn to creating? Write these down too and include what specific actions you will take to form these new habits.

Day 34

*"The cave you fear to enter
holds the treasure you seek."*

—JOSEPH CAMPBELL

My inner self or my soul voice has never been quiet about what she felt I should be doing. She always wanted me to be a writer. But for a long time, I was only able to approach that dream very tentatively.

After the experience of the women's writing group I wrote about on Day 23, I allowed myself little bits of writing, but it was always on the side. An internship at a weekly independent publication. Writing newspaper and magazine articles. A mentorship that led to writing and publishing short fiction. All of these things satisfied the urge to write, but that inner calling grew and the voice of my soul pushing me forward got louder.

By the time I was in my mid-thirties, I had not settled into any career path. I had a number of part-time jobs and told myself that I loved the variety. To anyone looking closely (and as I can see so clearly now in hindsight), it was obvious that the career I really wanted was the career I most feared, and therefore, I kept it at arm's length. I kept it on the side.

And then, out of the blue, the friendly universe intervened. I heard from an acquaintance who worked in the marketing department of a large organization. They were busy and needed to hire a freelance writer for a big project. She thought of me because she liked my newspaper writing.

I remember her emailing me details of the project. "Oh, and what's your rate?" she added. My rate? I had no idea. I quickly googled rates for professional writers, found a low number and a high number, chose something in the middle, and held my breath. She didn't bat an eye.

The job went well and it led to another one and another after that. Suddenly, I was freelancing, and I had a major client, one whose recommendation would help me get more work in the years to come. But I'm skipping ahead…

One day, I did the math. I figured out that using my new googled rate I could make more money writing than at all my other part-time jobs combined. The discovery of the external motivator of money suddenly gave value to my heart's desire.

DAY 34

Sad, I know, but that's what it took. I quit everything else and focused on the writing. That was two decades ago.

I can hear the universe chuckling about this as I write. It figured out a way to work with my fears and my stumbling blocks to make the life I wanted easier to say yes to. I know I'm not the only one who has had such an experience. The friendly universe gives us signs, leaves breadcrumbs on the path, and even steps in to make things happen.

But we have to be paying attention! To both the inner calling and then the help that arrives to push things along.

Julia Cameron of *The Artist's Way* says this:

"Once you accept that it is natural to create, you can begin to accept a second idea: that the Creator will hand you whatever you need for the project. The minute you are willing to accept the help of this collaborator, you will see useful bits of help everywhere in your life.... Learn to accept the possibility that the universe is helping you with what you are doing.... Expect the universe to support your dream. It will."

YOUR WRITING

Today, I want you to think about how the friendly universe might be pushing you along on your path. Here are some questions to guide your writing:

Are you paying attention to signs from the universe that you are on the right track? Write down what you are seeing, hearing, or experiencing that is in support of your dreams.

If you aren't able to see any specific signs yet, are there ways you could open to more assistance from the friendly universe? What would this look like?

Reflect on the inner callings that are surfacing as you've been reading this book. Write them down.

Day 35

*"Traveller, there is no path.
The path must be forged as you walk"*

—ANTONIO MACHADO

Yesterday, I wrote about how the friendly universe steps in to support our inner callings. Today, I want to take this one step further and pass along a piece of wisdom dispensed by Swiss psychiatrist Carl Jung. In 1933, he wrote a letter to a correspondent who had asked how best to live one's life. Jung said this:

> Your questions are unanswerable because you want to know how one *ought* to live. One lives as one *can*. There

is no single, definite way for the individual which is prescribed for him or would be the proper one.... But if you want to go your individual way, it is the way you make for yourself, which is never prescribed, which you do not know in advance, and which simply comes into being of itself when you put one foot in front of the other.

Later in the letter he advises that the letter writer do "with conviction the next and most necessary thing." This has been shorthanded to advice we've all heard—"one step at a time"—but I think Jung's wisdom is actually deeper than that.

He advocates the next and most necessary thing, not *any* step at a time. And in order to figure out the "most necessary" next step, we must tune in and allow ourselves to be guided. We need to be on the lookout for communication from the friendly universe in the form of intuitive nudges or synchronistic signs.

When I started to "make it" as a writer, I was stoked. I remember my accountant telling me that I was the only writer she worked with who made any money. I wore that as a badge of honour.

I had big clients and I worked on big projects and I loved it, until I began to feel subtly, and then not so subtly, unfulfilled. While I was doing what I loved for a living—working with words—many of the things I was paid to write were not terribly stimulating or creative. They also weren't written in my unique voice. Sometimes I was writing speeches on behalf of someone else or even books that had someone else's name on the cover.

And that's when my soul voice started to pipe up again. "Yes, you're a writer," I could hear her saying, "but you need to write your own stuff." She wanted me to write things from my heart, things that had more meaning. She also reminded me that I wanted to help other people.

At that time, there was a monastery nearby where I travelled for solitary retreats. This was the place I went when I wanted to be quiet and just "be" rather than "do." On one particular visit, I had an epiphany: I wasn't imprisoned in my career. Although I was successfully writing things for other people, I could also branch out and write things that invigorated and inspired me. And I could share them with others.

This was back in the day when you could easily launch a simple blogging website without bells and whistles. Over the course of two days, I chose my colours, picked some photos, and wrote my first blog post. I then committed to writing one blog post per week for a year. So many amazing things came as a result of this decision, including the book you're holding in your hands!

That year was one of the happiest of my life. I felt so alive and so creative. And the icing on the cake was the feeling I experienced when other people started to read what I was writing. Every week, more and more people signed up to receive my blog posts, and every week, more of them reached out to say that what I wrote resonated with them, touched them, or helped them.

This was the meaning I was looking for. I knew I was on the right track. Over the course of the next few years, I kept feeling for what the next and most necessary steps were. Based on that inner guidance, I gradually gave up most of my corporate clients. I also started designing writing challenges and programs and offering writing mentoring to people who wanted to create but felt stymied by their own self-imposed limitations.

My work began to feel more and more aligned with who I was at my core. This book is the next step on the path that I didn't plan but that makes perfect sense. It's the next and most necessary thing.

YOUR WRITING

Be on the lookout for insights or ideas that guide you to the next and most necessary step on your path. Use these questions to help you dive a bit deeper into the path you're on and the guidance you're receiving:

DAY 35

When I ask you what your next and most necessary step is, what is the first thing that comes to your mind? Write it down.

If it's all a bit hazy, but there are steps you can faintly make out, write those down too.

What emotions come up for you when you think about taking the next and most necessary step? Is there something stopping you? Write about what is keeping you from moving forward.

Day 36

*"Be patient toward all that is unsolved in your heart
and try to love the questions themselves,
like locked rooms and like books that are now written
in a very foreign tongue. Do not now seek the answers,
which cannot be given you because you would not be
able to live them. And the point is, to live everything.
Live the questions now. Perhaps you will then
gradually, without noticing it, live along some distant
day into the answer."*

—RAINER MARIA RILKE

When I first read this Rilke quote, I was in my late twenties. Having already spent most of my life being hard on myself, Rilke's advice—to be kind in the face of confusion and uncertainty—was a revelation. It had never occurred to me to try and have a peaceful heart when feeling lost or confused.

We live in a world where we are encouraged and rewarded for crafting elaborate floor plans, hammering out the details, and nailing things down. We aren't taught to listen within for next, necessary actions and patiently wait for our path to be revealed, one small step at a time.

Rather, we are told to hurry up and decide already. Take an aptitude test, look at a list of best paying careers, and choose one. Write your resumé, get an interview, get the job, and then stay there.

"Everything in our adult lives tells us that we should *know* where we're going, what we're doing, what it's all about," says American writer and artist Cynthia Morris. But, she adds, there is real value in not knowing and even in feeling lost.

"In the creative act, when you're making something, you have to surrender knowing and having everything figured out. Uncertainty is something children experience and that artists and creative people tap into daily. True power lies in our resourcefulness...in being able to figure it out and trusting ourselves."

Trusting ourselves. If this feels like a challenge, you're not alone. Fear and the critic piggyback on each other to convince us that we are not to be trusted, especially if we are doing something that might cause us to veer off the beaten path.

In some circumstances, where you feel comfortable or have a lot of experience, you might be okay with uncertainty. For instance, as a professional writer, I've learned not to panic when an article or a story is only half-done. Even if I'm stumped. I trust it will get finished and I will likely be happy with it. Why? Because I've been through the process enough times to know that I'm going to be able to see it through.

But what if you are between jobs? What if you've had a breakdown or a terrible breakup or you're sick? What if you know what you want to do but have no idea how to make it a reality?

These in-between states have higher stakes and can cause a sense of fragility. Trusting ourselves in these frightening and uncertain moments might be more difficult. There may be a tendency to be hard on ourselves. But we can practise turning the usual tormenting questions and statements on their head.

"Why haven't I figured this out already?" can be transformed into "There's no rush, I'm going to trust the process."

"I don't know what I'm doing" can become "I'm just going to try to love this big question mark and see what unfolds."

"I'm never going to get out of this" can turn into "I'm in an in-between place right now and it's not going to last forever."

Remind yourself that deep breaths and kindness are in order. If you can, think of any in-between time as an incubation period. Something is happening, you just can't see it yet. As you live the question, trust that the answer is on its way.

YOUR WRITING

Today, consider your own relationship with uncertainty, allowing these questions to guide you:

What is happening in your life right now that feels unresolved or like an open question?

Are you in an in-between place right now? Describe it. How does it feel? Be specific.

What areas of life do you trust yourself in? Where don't you trust yourself?

Write about how you feel in response to the "love the questions" approach.

Day 37

"Your resistance to change is likely to reach its peak when significant change is imminent."

—GEORGE LEONARD

A few summers ago, my neighbour spent a lot of time weeding and managed to get rid of all the goutweed in her backyard. Later, when we were talking over the fence, I congratulated her on her success. With a laugh, she said: "I did all that work and now, I've got horsetail! It's never-ending!" Having taken care of one invasive weed, she was faced with another.

Weeds are the perfect metaphor for all the things that stand between us and anything new and beautiful we are trying to grow or create. Your critic's judgments are the weeds in your garden. Your unexamined fears are the weeds in your garden. Too much screen time is a weed in your garden. We need to be vigilant to make sure the weeds don't crowd out what we have carefully planted.

When life is routine and uneventful, you may only have to deal with dandelions and clover, but, at the first hint that you're trying to accomplish something big, it's all goutweed and horsetail and never-ending mint.

As your 40-day adventure draws to a close, and especially if fresh insights or good ideas have taken root, you might find yourself besieged with more tenacious weeds in the form of increased fear, anxiety, and inner critic attacks. This is totally normal.

Anyone who has been on the cusp of a major life change or is involved in a meaningful, creative pursuit will understand this. Change makes us humans deeply uncomfortable and triggers a desire to keep things as they are. Anything new is perceived as scary, and we go into shutdown mode. We have to coax ourselves to open to this new, potentially frightening or intimidating thing. This could be going back to school, looking for a new job, ending a relationship, getting in shape, launching a business, or writing a book.

Building on our gardening analogy, in addition to weeding, we must also create an environment where those weeds can't get a foothold next time. We need to remember to fertilize the soil, place the plants in the sunlight, and feed them nutrients, water, and love. In other words, self-care! Making time for ourselves, listening to what we need, acting on what we hear, making appreciation lists, and tuning into the kind voice are vitally important. So are noticing and naming the critical voice and keeping fear out of the driver's seat.

This work might feel exhausting in the beginning—endless weeding, endless tending—but it does get easier. When I need a reminder, all I need to do is look over the fence. All of my neighbour's hard work has paid off in a gorgeous, thriving garden. The work is constant but necessary, and the payoff is incredible. Your future self, who is benefitting from all the work you are putting in now, will thank you.

YOUR WRITING

I'd like you to play with this metaphor of the garden using these questions:

What are you hoping *your* gorgeous, thriving garden will contain? What kinds of creations will it include?

What are you doing to nurture this new growth?

What are the weeds that get in the way?

How do you deal with these weeds?

Is there a way you could "up your game" when it comes to your gardening work? If so, set an intention for what you will do. Spell it out here in detail.

Day 38

"And the trouble is, if you don't risk anything, you risk even more."

—ERICA JONG

Impulsiveness gets a bad rap. Often associated with the very young or anyone diagnosed with ADHD, it is not considered a positive quality. Just google "impulsive actions" and you won't be greeted with stories of strangers helping each other in times of need or other random acts of creativity or kindness. All the top hits are about impulsive behaviour leading to "problems and regret" and "accidents and injury."

When you act on impulse, it means you act in the moment; you don't think about the consequences. I'd like to argue that this can actually work to our benefit, especially when it comes to our tender dreams, our most profound longings, and our creative ideas.

Of course, it goes against what we've been taught. We are encouraged to apply logic and intellect to our ideas, to "think things through" before acting, but we all know what happens when we're given too much time to think. Our inherent negativity bias, our fear of anything new, and our inner critic will all jump in and tell us why the status quo is so much safer and better.

Too much critical thought can be the kiss of death. Today, I'd like to recommend that more of us *should* act impulsively, especially when we feel an idea arising from an inner and true place inside of us. Think of it as one of the tools in your gardening box. Acting impulsively can help with our "weeding" work by not allowing fear and the critic to get a toehold.

What you have done in these last 38 days is to train yourself to listen within, to notice when the friendly universe is working in co-operation with you, and to begin to follow its hunches and signs and nudges. The next part of this work is to begin to honour and act on what you have discovered. And the most powerful way to honour what is within you is to protect it.

This means not letting the usual culprits wreak their havoc. By not giving fear and the inner critic the chance to join forces and bash your idea to the ground before you can take even a single, small step.

How do we do this? By acting quickly on our intuitive

DAY 38

nudges or soulful curiosities. You know the ones: to be on stage, to write a book, to take a painting class, to sign up for that course, to learn another language, to travel, to become an activist. These are prompts from your soul, helping you lean toward more meaning and more joy. More you.

Let's say you fondly remember acting in a play or a musical when you were in high school. You loved how alive you felt on stage and the feeling of kinship and connection with the cast and the crew. Over the years you've thought about your experience countless times and wondered about rekindling this old love by maybe joining a community theatre group. And then what happens? You shoot the idea down, telling yourself you're too busy or you're too old or you're not happy with your body shape. Does this sound familiar?

Next time you feel yourself being nudged or prompted, remember that you have three choices:

- you can ignore the impulse (fear and your inner critic are relieved and give each other a high five!)

- you can write it down as an idea to investigate on a to-do list (fear and your inner critic panic, do a quick huddle, and create a plan that ensures this item never comes off your to-do list)

- or you can immediately look up the website of a local amateur theatre group and before you lose your nerve, write them an email asking about auditions for upcoming shows or maybe opportunities to volunteer your time (fear and your inner critic look at each other in astonishment and slink into a corner to do some long-range planning)

This last option both respects the impulse *and* gets the ball rolling before those other not-very-kind/not-very-enlightened parts of us get in on the action.

YOUR WRITING

Today, I want you to write quickly in response to these questions before fear and your critic have a chance to jump in. Don't think too long or hard; just write!

What is something small you've been longing to do but have either felt stopped by fear or scolded by the critic?

What is something else that you really want to explore but you've told yourself a "story" about this particular thing (e.g., You don't have time, you're not talented enough, you're not in shape enough, etc.).

Now, take each of these longings and write down one small step you can take toward them TODAY.

And then do it!

Day 39

"We rise to great heights by a winding staircase of small steps."

—FRANCIS BACON

When you close the pages of this book, you will have amassed 40 days of a new habit, 40 days of new insights and ideas, 40 days of identifying and recognizing the things that are holding you back, and 40 days of becoming clear with how you want your life to change and what you want to create for yourself.

Your pockets may be bursting with seeds of new ideas. This might feel exciting. It might also feel overwhelming. So today, as you near the end of your 40 days, I want to propose something easy.

I don't want you to promise yourself that all of your brilliant ideas will become a reality. And I don't want you to pledge that you are going to make all of your dreams come true.

In the spirit of "the next and most necessary step," I only want you to commit to one thing: that you will keep this period of time for yourself. Keep the time of day you sit with this book and do your writing, whether that's early morning, late at night, or your lunch hour. Keep the same length of time that you currently use. Keep whatever cozy spot you have created—your desk, a comfy chair, or a beanbag. Keep it. Keep all of it. And keep going.

I'm telling you this now, before our time together is over, so you can prepare yourself to continue. Don't flag. Don't take a break. Don't stop. Don't let this time be just a blip in your life.

I want you to save this time for *you* rather than letting the time get taken up with something else. Don't let other responsibilities crowd in. Put this time in your calendar. Block it off.

Your happy challenge, once you've finished reading this book, will be to maintain the practice but to put your energy and time toward your heart's desires. How do you want to use this daily period of time? Later on, you can assess whether or not you need to add more time, change your location, or change the time of day when you do your work. For now, try to keep it the same so you have a sense of consistency.

DAY 39

If one of your innermost desires is to learn to play the piano, perhaps your "40-day" time becomes devoted to scales. If you've decided you want to become an activist, you could use this time to research the cause closest to your heart and begin to network. And if you want to write a book, this time could easily shift to working on your novel, your poetry, your memoir, or your short story ideas.

You have the momentum of a 40-day practice behind you. You can do this. You can keep it going. Keep showing up for yourself. Hold what you have learned about yourself dear and sacred. Honour it.

YOUR WRITING

Using what you have learned about yourself during this self-discovery process, I want you to set an intention about how you will use this time moving forward. Only you know what is in your heart to do.

Write in answer to these questions:

What will you dedicate this time to?

How will you keep this time sacred?

Who will you call on to support you? Who will you be accountable to?

Now, find a nice piece of paper and a pen and write a "shorthand" commitment/pledge to yourself and put it in a place you'll see it. You might also want to consider adding a goal that is within reach.

For instance, "I commit to 30 minutes a day at 7 AM to finish the short story I'm working on" or "I commit to an hour of playing guitar five days a week after work. My goal is to learn two new songs this month."

I suggest that you revisit and revise your commitments as you meet your goals.

Day 40

"Never give up, no matter how things look or how long they take. Don't quit before the miracle."

—ANNE LAMOTT

Every time I read a really good book, or discover a new song, or see a painting that moves me, or hear an inspiring TED Talk, I try to stop for a minute and just appreciate the bravery of the person behind it.

They overcame Resistance and dealt with their fears and prioritized their own self-care, all with the critic yelling loudly. They might have had to grapple with shame or unworthiness. They may have had trauma to heal. But they did it. And the world is a better place for their creation.

This is what I hope for you and for all of us. That the world will be a better place because of our creations.

Take a moment to congratulate yourself. Forty days is a long time, and this work is not for the faint of heart. Are you feeling pride in your accomplishment? Are you feeling excited or nervous about what's ahead? Are you feeling sad that your journey is coming to an end?

I hope with all my heart that you will look back on this time as the start of something truly beautiful. I hope this book is just the beginning of a much longer trek toward all that you are meant to create and gift the world. Keep tuning in. Keep taking the next and most necessary step. Keep following that golden thread as it unspools from your heart. Keep going. Keep going. Keep going.

YOUR WRITING

On Day 1, I asked you to create a snapshot of your life, including feelings, events, and curiosities. Today, reread that piece and then write about what has changed over these last 40 days. Be specific. Look for both small and large things, on the inside and on the outside. What is different? And why?

DAY 40

Second, I'd like you to write about your biggest insights or areas of growth from your entire 40-day process. What were your most profound learnings? What are you taking with you as you close the pages of this book? This exercise might take longer than one day, especially if you reread all of your writing from the last 40 days (which I highly recommend!).

Have fun and take your time.

DEAR READER,

Just like the grass that grows up out of cracks in concrete, our soul voice is tenacious and hardy. It doesn't stop talking to us. It doesn't stop prodding. Our inner knowing keeps patiently asserting itself until we begin to act.

I hope you are leaving this book ready to continue moving forward on your path. I hope your knapsack is full of handy new tools and nourishment that will sustain you. I hope you have found your inner compass and discovered it had been tucked in a safe hiding place all along. And I hope that you'll create your map as you go, stopping every so often, drawing in every new signpost, and giving thanks as you do.

If you enjoyed my book, if your own writing amazed you, or if your life has changed as a result of this 40-day adventure, please spread the word! This book is self-published and will be able to reach more people if you write an online review, and, of course, tell all your friends and your colleagues and your family and your book club and your writing group (etc! etc! etc!).

I would absolutely love to know how this book impacted you. Please write me with your stories!

And thank you for supporting an independent author!

With heart,

—Renée

RENÉE HARTLEIB
renee@reneehartleib.com
https://www.reneehartleib.com
Instagram: reneehartleib

GRATITUDE

My partner, Malve, for showing me doors where there once were only walls, for the strength I've found in her love, and for her faith in me.

My parents, Flo and Ray, for the foundation of love and books and possibility.

My sister, Lovena, for sharing the hatch and other adventures, and for walking the healing path with me.

My nephew, Tosh, fellow writer extraordinaire, for inspiring me with his writing, good questions, and soulful conversation.

Sadie, and the rest of my family—Ryan, Kai, Asha, Emmet, and Esja—for their presence, love, and support.

Elizabeth, for lighting this path and for accompanying me.

Gina, for her invaluable wisdom and advice.

Annemieke, for her kindness, sense of humour, and gorgeous design.

Marianne for her amazing eye and for pushing me over the finish line.

Mrs. Rutter, for spying the writer in me.

Melinda, for showing me what was possible.

Julia, for seeing me even when I was greatly disguised.

Denise and Danielle for holding my heart and my stories and for helping me to heal.

My friends who left too soon, Brenda and Stuart, and for all they taught me about living and dying.

All the women who have taken my workshops and all those who have trusted me with their stories and their books.

GRATITUDE

For long walks, deep talks, gentle support, and love: Kate M, Sister Kate, Anne B, Anne S, Colleen, George, Sherise, Les Féroces (Maggie, Jessie, Vanessa, Shelley), Lisa K, Janice, Binnie, Erna, Sarah E, Jess M, Sue A, Jane R, Andrea D, Sarah B, Amy, Cynthia, Elisabeth, Lis, and Lisa S.

There are many more who should be thanked, but too many to possibly name. Heartfelt appreciation to all those who have taught, guided, and supported me on all the steps of my path.

And, of course, thank you to the friendly universe, who, when I remember to trust, never fails to amaze me.

PRAISE FOR THE 40-DAY WRITING PROJECT

"I never realized how much time there was in an hour: Renée Hartleib's 40-Day Writing Project expands time, so that the 40 minutes (or however long) you commit to writing becomes (over 40 days) a year, a universe. It's a practical magic, and Hartleib's good advice and thoughtful stories give you the spell for it."

—SO MAYER, WRITER/ACTIVIST, LONDON, UK

"I looked so forward to the writing prompts each morning and love the richness and variety of material that Renée shares. It never failed to get me thinking and writing. And did I mention Renée is a beautiful writer? This is what initially drew me to this course, and I haven't been disappointed."

—MERYL COOK, WRITER AND ARTIST, NOVA SCOTIA, CANADA

*"I signed up because, although I love writing,
I needed a 'reason' to write. Like the dance classes
that I love and never make it to, like the sewing
machine that is one of my closest allies but sits most
often collecting dust on the shelf, my own writing
mostly didn't happen. Renée's writing project gave
me access to the kind of inner reflection I never
thought there was enough time for."*

—SUZY CROCKER, BOOKSELLER,
HALIFAX, CANADA

*"I have a long and maudlin history of taking part
in creative workshops/classes and feeling like
the least creative person in the room. You hear that
inner critic talking? The 40-Day Writing Project
gave me new tools for dealing with that voice and
hearing the others it tends to drown out. The exercises
Renée constructs are surprising, provocative,
useful and so nourishing that I expect to
keep returning to them over the next 40 years."*

—MADDY COSTA, WRITER, LONDON, UK

PRAISE FOR THE 40-DAY WRITING PROJECT

"When I embarked on this writing project I had no idea what to expect and was completely bowled over by the journey of self-discovery I found myself on. Renée's 40-Day Writing Project didn't just get me writing again, it got me thinking deeply about a huge variety of things in my life— past, present, and future. I experienced an incredible voyage, one that greatly boosted my self-love. Renée is a wonderful writer, and I feel so blessed to have stumbled across her and the magic she creates with her fresh approach to mentoring."

—LIZ BURNS, NOVA SCOTIA, CANADA

"This is a fantastic offering from Renée Hartleib. The daily prompts, from playful to deeply personal, delivered with thoughtfulness and generosity, have helped me create space in my life to explore and open up to my unique creative voice. I felt an immense impact early in the project that has continued to ripple out into my life."

—MAUREEN STRICKLAND,
MANITOULIN ISLAND, CANADA

"For me, the 40-Day Writing Project was like going on a long trip with myself, without taking any time off work. Renée's prompts are beautifully truthful and probing, causing unexpected things to spring from within, to see the light of day! I'm deeply grateful for this guided process, in all its gentleness and intensity."

—GEORGE WOODHOUSE, SINGER-SONGWRITER, NOVA SCOTIA, CANADA

"I started the project without thinking about it too much—and right from the first day, it seemed like someone inside of me had been just waiting for her chance! Renée's prompts are wonderfully inspiring and supportive. The exercises and the new daily routine have truly opened a new world to me. I highly recommend the project for anyone looking for new experiences and self-reflection."

—SANDRA SCHÜRMANN, CURATOR AND HISTORIAN, HAMBURG, GERMANY

PRAISE FOR THE 40-DAY WRITING PROJECT

"I enjoyed writing as a kid, and somewhere along my journey to adulthood I lost the joy in it. This project came along at the perfect time, allowing me to practise writing and find clarity. The daily prompts challenged me to explore and finish work on a deeply personal piece that I wouldn't have had the courage to write it if it was not for the 40-Day Writing Project."

—TYLER COLBOURNE, DARTMOUTH, CANADA

"A friend recommended this to me and I knew it was just what I needed—that little nudge to get started and get on a consistent path. Having a 'reason' to write every day instead of waiting for the feeling to strike was so helpful to me. I looked forward to each morning's prompt and wanted to get up early to spend that time with my thoughts and my pen."

—LISA WHITE, CPA, CA,
HALIFAX, NOVA SCOTIA, CANADA

"Last year, I gave myself an early birthday present. I would write for the 40 days leading up to my fortieth birthday. It was the best gift EVER! The 40-Day Writing Project was an opening that helped me find my confidence and gave me the courage to dare to softly whisper to myself: 'I am a writer.' One year later, I write. Renée's project was a catalyst for creativity, healing, and growth that continues to support me. So much gratitude for those 40 days that keep giving."

—CAROLE SURETTE, GRAND BARACHOIS, NEW BRUNSWICK, CANADA

Manufactured by Amazon.ca
Bolton, ON